Before "I Do"

Preparing for the Full Marriage Experience

By K. Jason Krafsky

Turn
the
Tide
resource group
www.FullMarriageExperience.com

Before "I Do" - Preparing for the Full Marriage Experience
Copyright © 2005 by K. Jason Krafsky.

Published by Turn the Tide Resource Group, LLC, 26828 Maple Valley Hwy #260, Maple Valley, Washington 98038. T3RG@FullMarriageExperience.com. 425.432.TIDE (8433).

Scripture verses throughout the book taken from *The Message*. Copyright © 1993, 1994, 1995, 1996, 2000, 2001, 2002. Used by permission of NavPress Publishing Group.

Scripture verses listed in the appendix taken from the *HOLY BIBLE, NEW INTERNATIONAL VERSION* ®. Copyright © 1973, 1978, 1984 by International Bible Society. Used by permission of Zondervan. All rights reserved.

Photographs from Jeff Culp Photography. Copyright © 2005 Jeff Culp. Used by permission. All rights reserved.

Although the author and publisher have made every effort to ensure the accuracy and completeness of information contained in this book, we assume no responsibility for errors, inaccuracies, omissions, or any inconsistency herein. Any slights of people, places, or organizations are unintended. Readers should use their judgment and consult clergy, professional counselor, or specialized relationship educator for more intensive relationship issues.

First printing 2005

For more information, resources, and updates, visit the website at
www.FullMarriageExperience.com.

ISBN 0-9769556-0-1

ATTENTION CHURCHES, COMMUNITY INITIATIVES, CORPORATIONS, COUNSELING AGENCIES, BOOKSTORES, NON-PROFIT ORGANIZATIONS: Quantity discounts are available on bulk purchases of this book for educational, gift giving, or fundraising purposes.

For information, please contact Turn the Tide Resource Group, LLC, 26828 Maple Valley Hwy #260, Maple Valley, Washington 98038. T3RG@FullMarriageExperience.com. 425.432.TIDE (8433).

Editing by Ken and Bekki Andersen
Proofreading by Lori Dilio
Cover and Design by Trudy Ferguson
Photographs by Jeff Culp
Production coordinated by Turn the Tide Resource Group, LLC

A portion of the proceeds from this book support groups involved in the emerging marriage movement, and efforts aimed to help people live authentic Christian lives.

Dedication

To the one I have been living
the Full Marriage Experience with since July 29, 1994.
Kelli, you are truly a gift from God.

Acknowledgements

Have you ever paid attention to acceptance speeches at the Oscars? The winner thanks anybody, everybody, and God for helping them get to that very moment. Most of the names are people the viewers have never heard of; yet, they are significant to the award recipient at a monumental moment in their life.

Writing a book is a big achievement. Publishing the book is just short of monumental. While I am not claiming any awards, nor assuming any are coming my way, I would like to acknowledge the people who helped make Before "I Do" become a reality. And in case this is my last opportunity to write a page like this, I am not holding back.

A laundry list of people have helped this marriage junkie with regular fixes of marriage information through their books, publications, speeches, web sites, programs and/or dialogue over phone, e-mail, or cups of coffee.

Thank you to Barbara Dafoe Whitehead, Barbara Markey, Diane Sollee, Maggie Gallagher, Bill Doherty, Wade Horn, Chuck and Barb Snyder, Michele Weiner-Davis, Bill Coffin, Roger Hillerstrom, Doug Engberg, Pat Fagan, David Olson, Julie Baumgardner, Focus on the Family, Greg & Candy McPherson, David Blankenhorn, Howard Markman, Greg Smalley, Tim Kimmel, David Popenoe, Gary Smalley, Linda Waite, Scott Sticksel, Les & Leslie Parrott, FamilyLife, Gary Chapman, Theodora Ooms, Norm Wright, Bill Bennett, Family Research Council, Michael and Diane Medved, Rozario Slack, John Trent, Mike and Harriett McManus, Tom Clifton, James Q. Wilson, Robert Rector, Don Browning, Chuck Colson, and many, many others.

Thank you to Jeff Kemp, the staff, the board, and the supporters of Families Northwest. Thank you for investing in me, and giving me the opportunity to help make the Northwest the world's premier place for marriage, family life, and children.

Over the years, hundreds of pastors have confirmed the need and desire for a book like this. Many of your names and faces floated in my mind as I endured through the stages of editing, rewriting, and publishing Before "I Do." Thank you for unknowingly prodding me.

I owe a special thanks to Dr. Scott Stanley, Natalie Jenkins, and the team at Christian PREP (Prevention and Relationship Enhancement Program) for granting their permission to adapt a portion of their tremendous work in sections four and five of Before "I Do."

I am grateful to the folks who cared enough to read the manuscript and offer their two cents (it was worth at least a million): Mark Zier, Glenn Stanton, David and Claudia Arp, Luke Nelson, Gary and Barbara Rosberg, Peter Larson, Pastor Dave Schaff, Pastor Charles Williams, Jerry and Janet Pryor, Pastors Rick and Jennifer Kraker, Pastor Kathy Perry, Carrie Abbott, Randy Hicks, Eric and Jennifer Garcia, and Ron Deal.

Before "I Do" is a reality today because Mark Eastburg first encouraged me to publish the book. Thanks Mark.

To Aaron Larson, thank you for your publishing insights.

I am especially grateful to Pastor Mitch Lomax, New Song Church, and the couples who field-tested Before "I Do" before I ever thought to do anything more with it.

I am indebted to the team of gifted people whose talents are all over this finished product, Ken & Bekki Andersen, Trudy Ferguson, Jeff Culp, and Lori Dilio. For a team on our first journey in book publishing, you all excelled like veterans in the field.

A special thank you to the couples that helped bring life to the ideas of the book by striking a pose. Thank you to Pastor Steve Murray, Martin Chang, Pastor Dave Waller, and Pastor Dan Larson for helping find some of those couples.

Thank you to American Printing & Publishing for producing the books. And thanks to Microgroove for all your work with the website, www.FullMarriageExperience.com.

To Pastor Ken Mitchell, the E-men, and our Community Group at New Community Church, thanks for your encouragement and prayers during the publishing process.

To the multiple Starbucks in spitting distance of my home, the guy who orders the *"grande coffee in a venti cup, double cupped, please"* thanks you for supplying a secondary office when I needed a quiet space to write.

When my wife and I were engaged, there were several couples that unofficially served as Marriage Investors to us. Thank you Kirk and Cindy Romberg, Duane and Geri Atkins, Bryan and Colleen Carter, and Steve and Tami Walker for letting us see there was such a thing as the *Full Marriage Experience*.

To Gram, I can't thank you enough for praying for me all of these years.

To my in-laws, Miles & Carolee, your lifelong commitment of marriage serves as a model not only for your daughter and I, but also to our four kids you call grandchildren.

To Caleb, Jaelyn, Josh, and Cole – each of you is a gift of God. I love you all and pray that you and your future spouses will live the *Full Marriage Experience*.

To Mom, thanks for your steadfast support and love which contributed greatly to making me the man, the husband, and the father I am today.

To my wife Kelli, I did, I still do, and I always will.

As a person who has been transformed by the love, the forgiveness, and the redemption of Jesus Christ, I thank Him for giving me purpose and hope.

(I hear the orchestra beginning to play the music, prompting me to quickly wrap things up.)

Finally, bringing this around full circle, thank you to you who is reading this page. You are either thinking about purchasing *Before "I Do,"* have already purchased it and are getting ready to go through it, or have gotten part way through the book and thought about reading this page. However it is that you are reading this page, thank you for bothering to pick up *Before "I Do."* It is designed to prepare you for the *Full Marriage Experience*, and I pray, that this book will help you live it.

What others are saying about, Before "I Do"

From Couples to Couples

"As a bride, you can spend so much time planning every detail of your wedding you may gloss over what it will mean to be married. *Before 'I Do'* allows you to invest time in details that will count the day after the "event" and for the rest of your life." **-- A**

"We believe that K. Jason Krafsky's pre-marital program is an invaluable first step for all marriages. The best part of *Before 'I Do'* was how it brought up subjects that we wouldn't have necessarily thought to discuss. We were able to discuss issues, come to agreements, and prevent possible future arguments." **-- M & J**

"*Before 'I Do'* is guy-friendly. It really helps you take baby steps towards talking about some issues that are hard for men to talk about." **-- J**

From the Experts to Couples

"*Before 'I Do'* will give you the Scriptural insights, knowledge and skills you need to make your marriage go the distance! This book is a must read before you say, 'I do!'" **-- David & Claudia Arp**, *co-directors of Marriage Alive International, authors of the 10 Great Dates Series including 10 Great Dates Before You Say "I Do"*

"*Before 'I Do'* is a marvelous way to prepare for the greatest journey in life – marriage. In *Before 'I Do,'* K. Jason Krafsky applies his wisdom and experience to helping couples set a clear destination, check and pack the essentials, leave unnecessary baggage behind, and, most importantly, make the clear decision if they really have the will to make the journey. I highly recommend his thoughtful and thorough approach." **-- Scott Stanley,** *Ph.D., author of The Heart of Commitment*

"*Before 'I Do'* is an excellent resource to help couples build a strong foundation for a lifelong healthy and happy marriage." **-- Aaron Larson,** *president of the National Healthy Marriage Institute, author of Long Distance Couples*

"Planning a wedding? Now, plan for a marriage! K. Jason Krafsky has put a valuable marriage tool right in your hands. Don't just fall in love, get prepared for it! Read *Before 'I Do.'*" **-- Ron L. Deal,** *president of Successful Stepfamilies, author of The Smart Stepfamily*

"Marriages will be happier, relationships more sound, and problems more manageable for couples who go through the superb pre-marital coaching in Jason Krafsky's *Before 'I Do'*." **-- Jeff Kemp,** *president of Families Northwest, former NFL quarterback*

"K. Jason Krafsky understands the unique challenges and fears this up-and-coming generation of couples face before and after the wedding day. He also knows what they need to overcome those obstacles. *Before 'I Do'* is his very beneficial effort to get that wisdom into as many couple's hands as possible and most importantly ... yours!" **-- Glenn Stanton,** *culture and research analyst, author of Why Marriage Matters*

From Couples to Marriage Investors

"While preparing for our marriage we appreciated a forum to discuss things that we hadn't thought to discuss (even in our 6 years of dating). *Before 'I Do'* is a helpful, easy-to-use format for setting a solid base for marriage."-- **M & J**

"The section, *Plan Your Life Together, Together* really exposed some major differences in the way we like to plan. It was a hard discussion to have, but just the awareness of our differences has been so important in our first few years of marriage." *-- **J & A***

From the Experts to Marriage Investors

"Before 'I Do' provides a theologically informed, fun, and in-depth review of the key issues premarital couples need to be considering. It's sure to help engaged couples build a solid foundation for a great marriage." *-- **Peter J. Larson, Ph.D.**, director of programs & outreach at Life Innovations, Inc.*

"I have conducted pre marital counseling for decades, utilizing the tools most of us as pastors and counselors had available. But I have to tell you, if K. Jason Krafsky's, *Before 'I Do'- Preparing for the Full Marriage Experience* was available then, marriages would have benefited from it's sound, biblical counsel and principles. Jason has hit the proverbial nail on the head! This new resource will impact generations to come with its thorough treatment of the importance of biblical preparation for marriage. I will coach my radio listeners, Divorce Proofing Campaign Partners, and reader's to use Jason's *Before 'I Do'* in their premarital counseling and to pass it along to pastors and counselors who are passionate about building biblical Truth into the couples they influence."
*-- **Dr. Gary and Barbara Rosberg**, founders of Divorce Proofing America's Marriages Campaign, authors of Divorce Proof your Marriage, co-hosts of "America's Family Coaches—LIVE!" (nationally syndicated radio program)*

"K. Jason Krafsky delivers a process that asks the right questions and prioritizes the key pre-marital/marital pieces of the puzzle. *Before 'I Do'* has direct application to the issues facing couples today and is a great tool for all of us working in marriage education." *-- **Eric & Jennifer Garcia**, co-directors of the Association of Marriage & Family Ministries*

"Before 'I Do' will be extremely helpful to those wanting to quickly start or enhance a marriage preparation program in their congregation."
*-- **Dr. Mark Eastburg**, executive director of Healthy Marriages Grand Rapids*

"In a time in which a wedding day is often little more than a 'prom on steroids,' K. Jason Krafsky has provided the faith community with a powerful tool for equipping couples to better prepare for lifelong marriage. *Before 'I Do'* asks all the right questions and presses all the right buttons, taking couples into a profoundly introspective experience that is enlightening, inspiring and practical."
*-- **Randy Hicks**, president of Georgia Family Council*

reface

My Journey to Discover the *Full Marriage Experience*

"When we get home, dad won't be there, and he isn't coming back."

I was just 11-years old when my older brother conveyed this information to me as he and my mom picked me up from a friend's house. The serious look on his face convinced me he wasn't joking. In my heart of hearts, I knew life was never going to be the same.

Like too many Generation-Xers, my happy home life shattered apart in the aftermath of my dad's grand departure. Everything changed. Child visitations quickly moved from weekly to monthly to non-existent. Finances tightened as child support payments followed the same pathway as the child visitations. Mom had to take on twice the responsibilities with half the resources. My brother and I struggled to cope with the swirling emotions of anger, pain, loss, and confusion. I remember praying, *"God, somebody somewhere has got to do something to keep this from happening to families."*

While my parents' divorce didn't destroy my desire to be a husband and father someday, it did spark a lot of questions. Through my teen years as I watched more of my friends' and schoolmates' families break apart, those questions turned to doubts.

  -- Will I leave my wife like my father did?
  -- How do I know if I will find the "right" woman?
  -- Will I cheat on my wife, or will she cheat on me?
  -- Do I know how to make a marriage work?
  -- Is there anything I can do to make sure my future marriage
    doesn't end in divorce?

These questions plagued me for many years. The answers seemed to be out of my reach.

And then, during my junior year of college, Kelli walked into my life. We hadn't dated long when we began talking about the "M" word. I needed answers to those questions ... and quick! But I discovered she was asking some of the same questions even though her parents had remained married.

For answers we read books, attended premarital classes, and went to a marriage conference. We talked to God and to ministers. We interrogated a number of couples who seemed to be happily married.

As these couples shared stories about their married life, the smiles, the twinkle in their eyes, and the affectionate glances gave it away: they were experiencing all marriage had to offer. Regardless of how long they had been married, I made three discoveries while listening to their stories.

First, married life is greater than they ever imagined. Secondly, marriage helped them discover more about themselves than they expected. Finally, marriage created a deeper appreciation for their spouse than they had anticipated.

The real life examples behind these lifelong love stories convinced me that marriage could be a lifetime adventure that is worth the journey.

Questions got answered. Doubt changed into hope. Anxiety turned into confidence.

Were these couples fortunate? Were they blessed? Did they know some special formula for success?

Well, kinda-sorta to all three.

Kelli and I got married on July 29, 1994. I have been a marriage junkie ever since. Thankfully, I have a day job that supports my habit.

I actually get paid to learn the latest and greatest information about marriage, family life, and relationships. Through my role at Families Northwest, I create community-based networks of relationship services and resources for couples, parents, and families. I also coordinate a marriage promotion campaign called *The Northwest Marriage & Family Movement*. The goal of the campaign is for marriages to be strengthened, parents to become more confident, and for fewer kids to be at risk of hearing "when we get home, dad won't be there."

Over the years, I have studied the age-old teachings from the Christian Scriptures, digested the findings from decades of social research, talked with the nation's smartest people on marriage, and listened to real life testimonies from countless married couples. I have examined most marriage and relationship books, surfed most marriage and relationship web sites, and reviewed numerous marriage enrichment programs. I have been trained in some of the best marriage/relationship programs that exist and participated in strategic discussions for national marriage efforts. I have counseled many couples, taught relationship basics to many more, and trained many, many pastors and leaders on marriage and family issues.

Through all my studies and work, one question lingers in my mind. How do the generations raised in a culture with too much divorce and too many broken families capture a vision for their marriage? How do they acquire a vision that helps them experience all marriage has to offer?

The *Full Marriage Experience* is the answer to that question. *Before "I Do"* was written specifically for pre-engaged, engaged, and newlywed couples to prepare themselves to live the *Full Marriage Experience*.

If my wife and I can live it, most anyone can.

When my dad abandoned our family, I knew my life was never going to be the same. I had no clue I would be where I am today. I never imagined God would use me to answer my own prayer.

If you are contemplating marriage, my prayer is that your questions get answered, any doubts change into hope, and your anxieties turn into confidence ... *Before "I Do"*.

-- K. Jason Krafsky

Table of Contents

Introduction

What is the *Full Marriage Experience*?

The *Full Marriage Experience* is to married couples what a map is to an explorer, what a nautical chart is to a ship's captain, and what architectural blueprints are to a builder. The map, chart, and blueprints are instrumental for those viewing them to reach their ultimate destination.

The *Full Marriage Experience* is instrumental for couples to reach their ultimate destination: to experience all marriage has to offer.

Couples need something greater than themselves in the times of laughter and pain, joy and sorrow, financial uncertainty, health troubles, and real life trials. By uniting around a common vision for their own marriage, and partnering with the Creator of Marriage, couples can endure through most anything, even circumstances that test their breaking point.

The *Full Marriage Experience* is that something greater couples need. The *Full Marriage Experience* results as one man and one woman unite and experience all ten ideals during their marriage journey.

E: Exchange a Lifetime Vow of Commitment

X: eXpand the Depths of Love and Intimacy

P: Protect and Nurture the Relationship

E: Endure Through Life's Highs and Lows

R: Raise and Teach Children

I: Interdepend on Each Other

E: Encounter God Together

N: Nurture Each Other's Well Being

C: Contribute to the Betterment of Society

E: Empower Others' Relationships

Millions of couples, hundreds of thousands of hours of research, thousands of years of experience, and hundreds of books (including *The Good Book*) confirm the *Full Marriage Experience*.

Great marriages are not the result of good luck, finding the perfect soulmate, or waiting for just the right moment. A great marriage is made, not born. To achieve a great marriage, couples must go into it with a clear purpose and clear intentions. The *Full Marriage Experience* is available to any couple that makes the commitment, acquires the knowledge, uses the skills, keeps the faith, and goes the distance!

Why Use Before "*I Do*"

An enormous amount of time is spent planning for the wedding day. Hours upon hours are spent picking out the perfect wedding cake, the prettiest flowers, and the most appropriate wedding announcements. Within a week of the wedding, the cake is eaten, the flowers are dead, and the invitations have been recycled. While they may all contribute to your special wedding day, they don't do much for the marriage.

Before "I Do" integrates proven relationship insights, Scriptural references, and practical relationship skills. Written from a Christian worldview, this guidebook displays a complete picture of what marriage is intended to be and how to get there.

Before "I Do" helps engaged and pre-engaged couples discuss issues, learn relationship fundamentals, and attain the skills to live the *Full Marriage Experience*. Couples benefit greatly by the topics covered, the issues raised, and the questions asked. While the book is filled with useful information, *Before "I Do"* engages readers to interact with the material, and more importantly, their mate.

The author makes no assumptions of who you are, what you believe, the family you were raised in, or the quality of your premarital relationship. Readers are welcome to disagree with any of the content in this book. But, while it is all right to have a difference of opinion with the writer, it is vital for you and your mate to be in full agreement on all things marriage.

I guarantee, after completing *Before "I Do"*, you will be prepared to live the *Full Marriage Experience*.

How to Use *Before "I Do"*

Before "I Do" is designed to help you and your mate discover more about yourselves and your relationship than you know now. This guide is adjustable to fit the schedules, the circumstances and fast-paced lifestyles of any couple.

Get the Books:
Each couple should have two copies of *Before "I Do,"* one for him and one for her.

Start Up:
The book is divided into eight sections. Each section is divided into seven-day chunks. Complete the first five days of exercises individually. On the sixth day, get together as a couple and discuss the material that you each completed on your own (using Couple Time Discussion Questions). On the seventh day, if at all possible, meet as a couple with a Marriage Investor to share comments, concerns, and issues that arise in each section.

Find a Marriage Investor:
Pre-marital education is fitness training for your relationship. *Before "I Do"* is an in-depth relationship fitness program. To increase what you get out of the "workout," meet with a Marriage Investor (clergy, small group leaders, marriage mentor, seasoned married couple, or counselor who acts as a pre-marital education facilitator). Meeting regularly with someone a little older and wiser will only enhance your pre-marital experience. They can provide perspective, accountability, and insights.

If you belong to a church or if your wedding is taking place at a church, meet with a pastor to find out about the congregation's pre-marital education opportunities. If they don't have a program, or their program does not include *Before "I Do"*, ask if they could help facilitate you and your mate through this book.

If you don't belong to a church, find one that offers *Before "I Do"* as its pre-marital education program (check out the Registry of *Before "I Do"* Providers at www.FullMarriageExperience.com).

Or you can turn to a trusted couple with a seasoned and healthy marriage. Order them their own copies of *Before "I Do"* and schedule times to get together and discuss the material.

For some, Christian counselors in your community may be the best option. Find a counselor who is willing to facilitate your pre-marital education experience with *Before "I Do"*.

Whoever your Marriage Investor is, check if they offer a relationship inventory (PREPARE or FOCCUS). It will help them help you even more.

If you have exhausted all routes to find a Marriage Investor and still come up short, go ahead and get started on your own.

Pace Yourselves:
The seven-day breakdown is only a suggestion (a strong one, but a suggestion nonetheless). Some may find finishing each section on their own over five days too slow of a pace. Feel free to go through the content faster. If it's too much work to complete the section in one week, break it up over two weeks.

Overcome the Distance:
If your relationship is long-distance prior to the wedding day (or engagement), complete the material as described above and plan regular phone dates to discuss each section. Reserve the time to discuss the section material only. Attempting to discuss other issues (such as wedding details) can either distract you from talking about your relationship or create tension by covering too many intense topics. In addition, arrange regular phone conferences with a Marriage Investor.

Go Deeper:
Every section has the potential to raise issues, questions, or information that may need more than what this book offers. Helpful books and articles, informative web sites, and practical resources related to topics covered in each section can be found at www.FullMarriageExperience.com.

Get Even More Out of *Before "I Do"*:
Create your own book club. If you have friends who are planning to get married (or planning to get engaged), coordinate regular times when all of you can get together and discuss the different sections of *Before "I Do"*.

Enhance Your Premarital Experience:
In some communities, churches work together to provide an array of programs to engaged and pre-engaged couples. Find out if there is a local weekend retreat, a daylong conference, or a series of classes that can complement your working through *Before "I Do"*.

Whether face-to-face or long-distance, get the most out of *Before "I Do"* by completing each section on your own, then discuss them as a couple, and then debrief as a couple with someone else. This is the time and season to invest as much as you can into your relationship to learn, discover, and discuss what you need to prepare to live the *Full Marriage Experience*.

Feel free to jot me an e-mail and let me know how things go.

K. Jason Krafsky
kjasonk@FullMarriageExperience.com

A Special Note for Marriage Investors
You play a pivotal role in the life of the couple in whose future marriage you are investing. That doesn't mean you have all the answers. Nor do you have to have had the "perfect" marriage. You simply need to be there for the couple. They need consistency, accountability, and someone who cares about their future marriage. At www.FullMarriageExperience.com is more information to help Marriage Investors, but here are a handful of tips to get you started.

Go Through *Before "I Do"* On Your Own:
Experience what the couple is going through by going through *Before "I Do"* on your own, or better yet, with your spouse. Even if you and your spouse are not conducting pre-marital education together, go through the book together. Take note of key questions throughout the sections. It will help you coach couples through the book.

Let *Before "I Do"* Do the Heavy Lifting:
Before "I Do" is a dynamic pre-marital guide that helps couples think about and discuss issues they have probably never discussed before. The process of discovery, introspection, and dialogue make this a constructive pre-marital experience. In your time with the couple, focus on key questions throughout the section, and inquire about what they learned about themselves and their relationship. This helps them articulate what they learned, which is a key step to move the knowledge from the head to the heart.

Use a Relationship Inventory:
If you are not using a relationship inventory in your work with engaged and pre-engaged couples, you are making your job a lot harder than it needs to be. PREPARE and FOCCUS are two similar but different relationship inventories designed to help Marriage Investors be more informed on the couple's relationship, more knowledgeable of strengths and growth areas, and therefore, more effective in their time with the couple. Different from personality and temperament tests, the relationship inventory allows you to have a broad assessment on how the couple feels about themselves individually, their mate, and their relationship. Find out more information and how you can get trained in a relationship inventory at www.FullMarriageExperience.com. The relationship inventories work hand-in-hand with *Before "I Do"*.

Make Adjustments (if Necessary):
Less is not more when it comes to pre-marital education. The eight sections in this book focus on the major relationship issues couples should know before the wedding day. If eight sessions with a couple is just not possible, pick and choose which sections are required and which sections are optional. Because relationships struggle and deal with different issues, use a relationship inventory to determine a couple's growth areas. This will allow you to personalize the required sections on where the couple has the greatest needs. Regardless of how often they meet with you, encourage the couple to complete the entire book before their wedding day.

Get Help (It's Just a Click Away):
The web site offers an ever-expanding list of helpful tips, ideas and resources to assist Marriage Investors. Check it out often. If you don't find the answers you need, e-mail your questions to me (kjasonk@FullMarriageExperience.com).

Promote Your Pre-marital Services to the World (or at least your area):
If *Before "I Do"* is your primary pre-marital education tool, promote your church or organization on the Registry of *Before "I Do"* Providers at www.FullMarriage-Experience.com. It's free, it's easy, and it's a no-brainer. You benefit from the national promotion and sales of this book. This is a simple way for couples in your area to find the pre-marital education they want, and that you can provide.

I welcome your e-mails as we embark together to help more couples live *the Full Marriage Experience*.

K. Jason Krafsky
kjasonk@FullMarriageExperience.com

Section 1

Lay the Foundation for a Lifelong Marriage

Today, when a couple announces, *"We're getting married!"* they unwittingly open themselves up to loads of advice, opinions, and comments from every Tom, Dick, and Harriet.

Unbeknownst to this innocent pair, they have opened the door for family members, friends, acquaintances, and perfect strangers to offer their two cents' worth of advice on marriage, relationships, divorce, family planning, and other related topics. In some cases the advice may not be worth the two pennies. Or, it may be worth more than all the worlds' fortunes.

What makes a marriage great? How can a couple keep the love sparks ignited? What does it take to be a good husband or wife? How can a couple ensure their marriage will go the distance? Do they have what it takes for their marriage to last a lifetime?

Before any of these questions can be answered, a more elementary question should be asked. What is marriage? How one defines marriage reveals a lot. The couple's response exposes the foundation on which a couple is building their marriage.

This first section, **Lay the Foundation for a Lifelong Marriage,** helps couples take the first steps towards the *Full Marriage Experience.* Couples will gain a deeper understanding of marriage and the fundamentals for this one-of-a-kind relationship. This section will also lay the groundwork for the rest of the sections in *Before "I Do".*

> *In the space provided below, list the best pieces of advice you have heard for married couples?*

DAY ONE

What's Your Foundation?

marriage factoid

-- Nearly nine in ten Americans will get married at some point in their life.

-- The average first marriage age is 25 years for women and 27 years for men.

-- Nearly two-thirds of all first marriages will succeed in lasting a lifetime.

take a note

Faulty Foundation

A shallow foundation for a marriage that rests on emotionally-based reasons that are unable to support a couple through trying times.

Separate Foundations

Two different foundations that result when a couple possesses conflicting definitions or reasons for their marriage. Over time, the gap between the two foundations becomes more obvious, and the impact on the quality of the relationship more severe.

Couples decide to get married for a variety of reasons: they love each other, they want to spend the rest of their life together, they are best friends, and/or they want to start a family together.

Marriage is something many couples want, but do they know what marriage really is? In a day and age when one out of three first marriages ends in divorce, couples must have a common definition of marriage, agree on its purpose, and know the fundamentals to keep it healthy.

Everyone knows couples who have walked down the aisle and become husband and wife. How many of them are still together? Of those who divorced, how long did their marriages last? What contributed to the breakdown of their marriage?

Chances are these couples were doomed to fail from the very beginning, but not because they were victims of bad luck, the divorce curse, or random acts of unkindness. In many cases, couples build their marriage on either a *Faulty Foundation* or *Separate Foundations*.

A *Faulty Foundation* lacks the depth that can sustain long-term conditions. The reasons for marriage cited at the top of this page can act as a couple's marriage foundation. Unfortunately, they can also become a couple's reason for a divorce. The couple may "fall out of love," drift emotionally apart, head down opposite career paths, or experience trauma with their child (illness or death).

Separate Foundations result when the couple possesses conflicting definitions of marriage. Many people define marriage as a lifelong commitment that withstands the ups and downs of life. Others believe marriage to be a relationship that is valid only as long as love shall last. Still others believe marriage should be whatever whoever wants it to be for however long they think it should last. When a couple believes different ideas about marriage, they have laid *Separate Foundations*.

The **Foundation for a Lifelong Marriage** raises the standard to a higher level. It brings out the best in the couple and motivates the husband and wife to strive for their personal best. It is an indestructible foundation that breeds confidence in both the man and the woman.

The Chief Builder and Architect of marriage created three ingredients for the *Foundation for a Lifelong Marriage*: **God's Four-Fold Vision for Marriage**, a **Five-Dimensional Love**, and a **Covenant Commitment for Marriage**. Each ingredient displays God's purpose and His divine intentions for marriage.

Do you have concerns that your marriage could be built upon a Faulty Foundation or Separate Foundations? Why or why not?

Share ingredients you think are important for the foundation of your future marriage.

God's Four-Fold Vision for Marriage

DAY TWO

God's Four-Fold Vision for Marriage is revealed in the first two chapters of Genesis. God created marriage with four distinct and interrelated purposes. Any couple considering a lifetime together should be fully aware of *God's Four-Fold Vision for Marriage.*

1. Marriage is *A Living Advertisement for God.*

Men and women are made in God's image. Together as husband and wife, the man and woman reflect God's nature. Throughout married life, the two halves of humanity showcase God's love, joy, mercy, grace, sensitivity, tenderness, care, forgiveness, and commitment.

When a couple engages in the act of marriage, they display God. How couples handle life's ups and downs presents a side of God's nature to the world. How a couple communicates, argues, and resolves conflict give people a greater sense of who God is.

By uniting both parts of humanity, marriage helps people grasp God better, see God more clearly, know God more deeply, and live for God more intently.

Every married couple is an advertisement for God. Ultimately, it is up to each married couple to decide how persuasive their public notice for God will be.

In what ways will your marriage advertise God to the world?

How persuasive will your marriage be as A Living Advertisement for God? Why?

2. Marriage is *The Ideal Family Environment.*

God yearns to be in relationship with as many people as possible. Therefore, He desires husbands and wives to become moms and dads.

Because women and men have diverse and balancing strengths, both are essential and needed to raise children. Marriage provides the natural forum for procreation and the natural set of caretakers for children.

Four decades of social science research shows that children are more likely to thrive emotionally, academically, physically, spiritually, and socially when they are raised with their married mother and father.

the Bible says

"God spoke: 'Let us make human beings in our image, make them reflecting our nature so they can be responsible for the fish in the sea, the birds in the air, the cattle, and, yes, Earth itself, and every animal that moves on the face of the Earth.' God created human beings; he created them godlike, reflecting God's nature. He created them male and female."
Genesis 1:26-27

the Bible says

"God blessed them: 'Prosper! Reproduce! Fill Earth! Take charge!'"
Genesis 1:28a

Children raised by their married mom and dad gain a healthy appreciation and balanced understanding of the two genders. Because moms and dads bring different perspectives to the table, kids gain a more complete understanding and view of the world.

Mothers and fathers parent differently, play with the kids differently, communicate differently, discipline differently, and prepare children for life differently. But it's not just about the kids. The shared objective to raise and teach children allows couples to experience new dimensions in their own relationship.

Sprouting new branches from the newly grafted family tree provides future generations a stable foundation and secure identity. For people raised in a less than ideal family environment, starting a family gives them the opportunity to learn from their past and establish a new family environment for their own kids' sake.

■ *Do you plan to have children? Why or why not?*

■ *List a few of the "diverse and balancing strengths" you and your mate possess from which your future children will benefit.*

3. Marriage is *An Essential Societal Institution.*

The cornerstone for every stable and robust society has been marriage. When a man and woman assume the legal and societal commitments to become husband and wife, they expand the web of natural caretakers for fellow citizens within a society. Marriage serves the common good for communities and society in irreplaceable ways.

Since the beginning of time, most civilizations, governments, and major religions have sanctioned this vital institution because of its wide sweeping benefits. Marriage produces healthier individuals, more stable households, wealthier families, and the most natural structure to care for children. No other relationship or family formation impacts society as positively as marriage does.

Children raised in a healthy married home are likely to replicate their positive family experience. A healthy marriage influences the next generation, which results in multiple generations of healthy family relationships. A husband and wife make the difference whether their marriage and family is an asset or a detriment to society.

Society has a vested interest in the success of each and every marriage. This is why, through helpful policies and benefits, society supports, encourages and protects marriage.

Society has a vested interest in the success and well-being of your future marriage. How does this affect you?

Assuming you will have children, what kind of family life do you desire for your great, great grandchildren? How can your marriage today influence them generations from now?

4. Marriage is *The Ultimate Couple Relationship.*

God designed marriage to be like no other relationship on earth. It had to be the perfect combination of qualities causing men and women to yearn for it. It had to provide an array of unique benefits to motivate couples over the course of a lifetime together. It had to raise the standard to help men and women attain a quality of relationship that they couldn't get anywhere else. It had to be the ultimate of all relationships.

He succeeded! God handcrafted the relationship to blend complementary strengths, deep intimacy, lifelong permanence, and mutual acceptance.

-- Marriage is God's prescription to complement the other. Knowing that both the man and woman have different strengths and weaknesses, God prescribes His divine help to both the husband and wife. Every couple possesses irreconcilable differences before, on, and after the wedding day. But rather than dividing the couple, these differences are intended to unite them.

-- Marriage is God's designed sanctuary for deep intimacy. Sex was created to be enjoyed and celebrated within the safe sanctuary of marriage. The God-given sex drives can be unleashed after a couple has devoted their sexual longings exclusively to one another in the wedding ceremony. When a couple protects their hearts, minds, and bodies prior to the wedding day, they are more likely to enjoy sexual intimacy more often, and at a deeper level over the course of their lifetime together.

-- Marriage is an inseparable union in which one man and one woman choose to create a permanent bond. The exchange of "I do's" is more than a simple promise. When a couple unites, it is like an industrial stength adhesive bonds them together. This union is not intended to be broken.

-- Marriage is a safe harbor to nurture unconditional acceptance. Being in a lifelong relationship builds personal security and well being. It encourages spouses to live their life for another. As a result of sharing their lives, their bodies, their successes, and their failures, a husband and wife come to know each other so well that no shame exists between them.

worthy quote

"... in marriage you are placed at a post of responsibility towards the world and mankind... marriage is more than something personal – it is a status, an office. Just as it is the crown, and not merely the will to rule, that makes the king, so it is marriage, and not merely your love for each other, that joins you together in the sight of God and man."
-- **Dietrich Bonhoeffer**, *German pastor killed by Nazis*

the Bible says

"God said, 'It's not good for the Man to be alone; I'll make him a helper, a companion.' So God formed from the dirt of the ground all the animals of the field and all the birds of the air. He brought them to the Man to see what he would name them. Whatever the Man called each living creature, that was its name. The Man named the cattle, named the birds of the air, named the wild animals; but he didn't find a suitable companion. God put the Man into a deep sleep. As he slept he removed one of his ribs and replaced it with flesh. God then used the rib that he had taken from the Man to make Woman and presented her to the Man. The Man said, 'Finally! Bone of my bone, flesh of my flesh! Name her Woman for she was made from Man.' Therefore a man leaves his father and mother and embraces his wife. They become one flesh. The two of them, the Man and his Wife, were naked, but they felt no shame."
Genesis 2:18-25

Marriage provides men and women the opportunity to experience deep levels of intimacy, companionship, security, and mutually-beneficial support and care. Marriage is a relationship that is second to none.

■ ***How does marriage differ from a dating or unmarried cohabiting relationship?***

■ ***What part of The Ultimate Couple Relationship are you most looking forward to?***

God's Four-Fold Vision for Marriage

1. A Living Advertisement for God

2. The Ideal Family Environment

3. An Essential Societal Institution

4. The Ultimate Couple Relationship

God has a tremendous vision for marriage. As a result of divine design, marriage benefits women, men, children, families, communities, societies, nations, and future generations.

To experience the fullness of what marriage is and can be, couples should align themselves with *God's Four-Fold Vision for Marriage*. Couples who attempt to create their own vision for marriage usually fall short of attaining their hopes and dreams. The first ingredient of the *Foundation for a Lifelong Marriage* is *God's Four-Fold Vision for Marriage*.

■ ***How have your thoughts on marriage changed or expanded after reading God's Four-Fold Vision for Marriage?***

■ ***What is your vision for your marriage?***

A Five-Dimentional Love

DAY THREE

Our society is in love with the word "love."

--A Google search brings up 71 million hits (e.g. "the love bug" virus, advice on finding love, and Uncle Pedro's House of Naughty are a few examples).

--Popular radio programs play hours of dedicated "love songs."

--Magazine covers at the grocery store beckon readers with headlines proclaiming how to find, keep, spice up, and let go of love.

--After each show, Barney the purple dinosaur shares how he loves you, you love him, and magically it makes the viewing audience and Barney a happy family (sealed with a "great big hug and kiss" from him to you).

Love is one of the vaguest terms in the English language. In Webster's Dictionary alone there are over 24 different definitions for this one word. Add a letter or two to the end and there are many more. This single four-letter word can be a noun, a verb, and with a little change, can become an adjective and an adverb as well.

In today's culture, the word is used interchangeably in all kinds of expressions: "I love it," "I love you," "I'd love to go."

How do you define love?

Where does love come from?

Do you believe love is more feeling or decision? Why?

How can a person foster love for their spouse over a lifetime?

worthy quote

The responses from kids who were asked, "What are people thinking when they say 'I love you.'"

"They're thinking, 'I sure love Mary. I hope Mary loves me too. Because if she don't love me, I'm going to have the world's biggest heartache and a giant headache to go with it.'"
-- Kenneth, age 10

"Oh my gosh, I'm in love...What will my mother say?"
-- Sharon, age 9

"The person is thinking, 'Yeah, I really do love him. But I hope he showers at least once a day.'"
-- Michelle, age 7

"People who say, 'I love you' are too silly to be thinking anything at all."
-- Gerard, age 6

The languages in Biblical times had distinct words for the different meanings of love. Five terms were used to describe different aspects of love. This clarified whether people were expressing love for someone or something. There was no confusion when a person said "I love you" to their spouse, their friend or their mother.

Understanding the five different dimensions of love broadens a couple's view of how deep love really is and what it takes to live it out. A **Five-Dimensional Love** is the second ingredient of the *Foundation for a Lifelong Marriage*.

Devotion

Devotion is the loyalty to one another that grows and strengthens with every day the couple is together. It is connected with *"that feeling like we have been together forever."* Although it may not have the emotional peaks of some of the other dimensions, it is equally important and vital to the longevity and health of a marriage. It brings with it a sense of loyalty, belonging, security, and comfort.

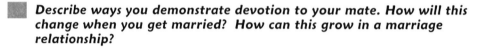 *Describe ways you demonstrate devotion to your mate. How will this change when you get married? How can this grow in a marriage relationship?*

Camaraderie

This describes the type of love between best friends, constantly building camaraderie between the two. It is a love that cherishes another person, has tender affection towards another, and is developed by spending time together, getting to know the person for who they are, and building a trust and respect for the other.

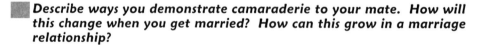 *Describe ways you demonstrate camaraderie to your mate. How will this change when you get married? How can this grow in a marriage relationship?*

Passionate Desire

This dimension of love describes an aspect of the physical and emotional relationship between the husband and wife. It is to have a strong craving for the other, to desire one's mate at a physiological level, or to passionately long for one's spouse. Having passionate desire for one's spouse is the springboard for mutually pleasing one another. It is the fuel for pleasurable lovemaking and intimacy.

Describe ways you demonstrate passionate desire to your mate. How will this change when you get married? How can this grow in a marriage relationship?

"I am my lover's. I'm all he wants. I'm all the world to Him!"
Song of Solomon 7:10

Romance

Romance is the love that delights in one's spouse and in the relationship. It is an emotional experience that takes pleasure in the way a spouse looks and feels and in what they say and do. It is as if the love one has for another is boiling over. Romance bridges the platonic and practical aspects of love with the passionate aspects of love.

Describe ways you demonstrate romance to your mate. How will this change when you get married? How can this grow in a marriage relationship?

"Come, dear lover – let's tramp through the countryside. Let's sleep at some wayside inn, then rise early and listen to bird-song. Let's look for wildflowers in bloom, blackberry bushes blossoming white, fruit trees festooned with cascading flowers. And there I'll give myself to you, my love to your love."
Song of Solomon 7:11-12

a closer look

First Corinthians 13:4-8 includes these elements of unconditional love:

--Never gives up
--Cares more for others than for self
--Doesn't want what it doesn't have
--Doesn't strut
--Doesn't have a swelled head
--Doesn't force itself on others
--Isn't always "me first"
--Doesn't fly off the handle
--Doesn't keep score of the sins of others
--Doesn't revel when others grovel
--Takes pleasure in the flowering of the truth
--Puts up with anything
--Trusts God always
--Always looks for the best
--Never looks back
--Keeps going to the end

Unconditional Love

This is the most talked about love in the New Testament because it is the type of love God demonstrates towards humankind. The most popular passages on unconditional love are found in I John 4 and I Corinthians 13.

This is a love based on total acceptance of the other despite the person's faults. It is an unshakable commitment to care for another. To love in this way is to love with grace, mercy, favor, and commitment regardless of the person's responsiveness or if they show reciprocal behavior.

Unconditional love is mandatory for a husband and wife to live *the Full Marriage Experience*.

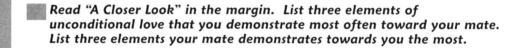 *Read "A Closer Look" in the margin. List three elements of unconditional love that you demonstrate most often toward your mate. List three elements your mate demonstrates towards you the most.*

From the list in the margin, list three elements of unconditional love that you demonstrate the least toward your mate. List three elements your mate demonstrates towards you the least.

Living out unconditional love demands actions, behaviors, and attitudes out of people that transcend momentary feelings. This type of love demands more than mere lip service. This is not a love for wimps. It is a love that forces a person to give all they have to offer and then some. Words that describe unconditional love include selflessness, servant-mindedness submission, and sacrifice.

▪ *Describe ways you can show unconditional love to your mate. What can you do to demonstrate this in your marriage relationship?*

▪ *What are the personal challenges to showing someone else unconditional love?*

Marriage is the only relationship in which all five dimensions of love are displayed. To exist in the polar regions of love causes disharmony and dysfunction in the relationship. If love remains only at the biological or emotional level by a couple attempting to keep the "in love" feelings, that relationship has a short lifespan.

Picking and choosing the facets of love one wants, and leaving the others behind, deprives a marriage relationship of experiencing love to the depths that is humanly possible. God's design blends all the dimensions together to form a strong bond, like cords wrapped together provide to a rope.

To experience love at deeper levels, to witness love in day-to-day life, couples must expand and broaden their view of what love is. Otherwise, couples risk missing out on the richness and fullness of what God has in store for their life and for their marriage.

Expressing a *Five-Dimensional Love* in marriage is central for a couple to live the *Full Marriage Experience*.

▪ *Do you believe you have the ability to show your mate a Five-Dimensional Love for the rest of your life? Why or why not?*

marriage factoid

"A five-year study found that continuously married people experience better emotional health and less depression than do never-married, remarried, divorced or widowed individuals. The study also reported that getting married for the first time significantly increases a person's emotional well-being."

-- The Family Portrait

take a note

A Five Dimensional Love:

--Devotion
--Camaraderie
--Passionate Desire
--Romance
--Unconditional Love

Joining with *God's Four-Fold Vision for Marriage*, a *Five-Dimensional Love* is the second ingredient of *the Foundation for a Lifetime Marriage*.

DAY FOUR | Covenant Commitment For Marriage

The term "covenant" describes the marriage relationship throughout the Bible. A concept foreign to modern times, the closest western culture comes to the idea of covenant is with the term "contract."

A contract is a temporary agreement between two or more parties to give something in exchange for receiving something.

Contracts are a part of everyday life. A contract must be signed between a landlord and tenant. A contract is signed between employers and employees agreeing to terms, compensation, benefits, and work policies. Some couples sign a contract prior to getting married (prenuptial agreement) as a way to protect their personal assets in case of divorce. Some couples sign a contract to protect personal assets acquired after the wedding day (post-nuptial agreement).

Contracts can be a good thing in life, but they are limited. They can be changed, ignored, and broken. The motivation to break a contract ranges from dissatisfaction with the terms, inability to pay, or disagreement with the other party. Contracts are broken regularly in today's society.

The idea of covenant is very different. A covenant is two parties mutually entering into an unconditional, life-long promise that cannot be broken. Regardless if one of the two parties neglects to fulfill their part of the agreement, the covenant is still binding.

In the Old Testament, several covenants are recorded between God and mankind. Always present when a covenant was made were witnesses and a visible seal that would remind the parties of the covenant.

Couples can have a *Contract-Based Relationship*. The thought pattern goes like this: *"If you give me something, I will give you something. If you stop giving something to me, I will stop giving back to you."* The contract can be based on monetary stability, sex, social status, companionship, or security. *Contract-Based Relationships* tend to last only a little while. Inevitably, one party defaults on their end of the bargain resulting in devastation for any marriage. Sometimes a spouse may not realize the other is considering their marriage as a *Contract-Based Relationship*.

A marriage established as a covenant brings a whole new meaning to the word commitment. A **Covenant Commitment for Marriage** (defined in the margin) has the best interest of the other person in mind, regardless of their actions, their weaknesses, and their frailties. It does not expect perfection out of the other partner. It does, however, anticipate perseverance. And with this sort of selfless-driven commitment, time enhances trust and boosts the levels of dedication, ultimately resulting in a deeper love and admiration for the other.

Today, marriage is one of the weakest, non-binding contracts that exists. The responsibility to bolster the relationship to a *Covenant Commitment for Marriage* falls on the couple. To determine their ability to commit, each person must look at their personal record of keeping promises and fulfilling obligations, and assess it in light of their future vows.

take a note

Contract-Based Relationships:

A temporary agreement between two people establishing a relationship based on giving something in exchange for receiving something in return.

Covenant Commitment for Marriage:

A man and a woman mutually entering into a marriage relationship based on an unconditional, lifelong vow before God and witnesses to love one another, care for one another, and be faithful to one another until death separates them.

the Bible says

"...God was there as a witness when you spoke your marriage vows to your young bride ... your vowed companion, your covenant wife. God, not you, made marriage. His Spirit inhabits even the smallest details of marriage. And what does he want from marriage? Children of God, that's what. So guard the spirit of marriage within you."
Malachi 2:14-15

Promises Kept, Promises Broken

Remember how important keeping a promise was in grade school? Playground secrets prevailed and before one put their confidence in telling another a secret, the question inevitably was asked, "*Can you keep a secret?*" A simple "*I promise*" would not hold up.

Kids were required to cross their heart, hope to die, and promise to stick a needle in their eye. They were also required to swear on their mother's reputation or commit to eat a bowlful of the grossest concoction a ten-year old could dream up. Then, and only then, could the secret be told: "*Emily likes Jacob. But don't tell anyone.*"

In the teen years, reputations, friendships and relationships all hinged on whether someone could be trusted and keep their word. Friendships where promises were kept typically grew deeper. Those that could not, did not.

In adult life, the importance of keeping one's word has great value and holds a greater threat of consequences.

> *In the checklist below, mark how well you have kept your promises to others. If you have kept your promise (word, obligation, commitment), mark the statement as "Kept." If you have broken any example just once, mark it as "Broken."*

	Kept	Broken
Taking a test in school without cheating or copying.	☐	☐
Making house/apartment payment on time.	☐	☐
Paying the IRS with the correct amount of taxes owed.	☐	☐
Repaying student loans (or all other debts) on time.	☐	☐
Being truthful to parents throughout teen years.	☐	☐
Performing all obligations to current employer or boss.	☐	☐
Showing up on time and in the right place to meet mate.	☐	☐

> *Estimate how often you keep your promises to others (use percentage).*

> *In your opinion, how important is it for a person to keep their promises? How important is it for you to keep your promises?*

> *How do you feel when a person breaks a promise they made to you? What do you feel towards that person?*

marriage factoid

Celebrity marriages have always made the headlines of Hollywood rags. In recent years, the shorter the marriage, the longer the coverage. Here are the names of celebrities followed by the amount of time between their wedding day and splitting day.

--Jennifer Lopez & Cris Judd (9 mos.)
--Drew Barrymore & Tom Green (5 mos.)
--Nicolas Cage & Lisa Marie Presley (3 mos.)
--Katherine Hepburn & Ludlow Ogden Smith (3 weeks)
--Dennis Rodman & Carmen Electra (9 days)
--Zsa Zsa Gabor & Felipe de Alba (1 day)
--Rudolph Valentino & Jean Acker (6 hours)

worthy quote

"*Tell me the worth of a society where it is easier to get a marriage license than a fishing license. Tell me the sense of a society where it is easier to get out of a marriage contract with children than it is to get out of a Tupperware contract.*"
-- **Frank Keating**, *former Governor of Oklahoma*

DAY FIVE

Traditional Wedding Vows:

"I solemnly vow before God and our family and friends, to be your loving and faithful wife/husband. I vow to love you, to honor you and to be faithful to you; in times that are for better or for worse, for richer or for poorer, in sickness and in health until my final breath. I take you to be my husband/wife."

"When a man makes a vow to God or binds himself by an oath to do something, he must not break his word; he must do exactly what he has said."
Numbers 30:2

"If you say you're going to do something, do it. Keep the vow you willingly vowed to God, your God. You promised it, so do it."
Deuteronomy 23:23

"An impulsive vow is a trap; later you'll wish you could get out of it."
Proverbs 20:25

The *Promises Checklist* can be a humbling endeavor. When faced with the facts from brutally honest responses, everyone has broken at least one promise, or failed to keep a commitment in their life. Whether towards those we care deeply about, or people we hardly know, breaking promises reveals one's frailty.

The moment one realizes they are incapable of keeping their word, their reaction is to make excuses. *"Everyone does it." "No one is perfect." "The rules were not fair." "No one got hurt." "It was easier than telling the truth." "He/She didn't have to know about it." "It's easier to ask for forgiveness than to ask permission."*

The realization of one's inability to perfectly keep their word does not have to be solely an admission of weakness. It can be a great motivator. When a person knows they are capable of breaking promises and failing to keep commitments, they typically give greater heed to their words and more thought to their pledges. This should be the reaction to every prospective bride and groom.

A Look at the Vows

Every wedding day, couples make their vows before friends and family. The vows are not simply a promise until feelings change. The vows establish a covenant relationship between the husband, wife, and God.

Most people can recite the traditional wedding vows exchanged by the bride and the groom.

All the elements of establishing a covenant are involved in the wedding ceremony: the parties (man-woman-God), unconditional, life-long promise (marriage vows), witnesses (God and friends), and the visible reminder of the covenant (exchange of rings).

Too often, couples recite the vows without the sober realization of what living out the vows will demand of them. Read the three Bible passages in the margin and then continue.

■ **How does God view your making a vow to Him? Why do you think He takes such a strong stand?**

■ **Why is it a trap to make a vow and only later consider its significance?**

For some people, their wedding day is the day they enter into "a trap." They do not consider the significance of their vows until after the fact.

The severity of the vows and the length of the commitment doesn't have to take people by surprise. Each person has a certain view about the longevity of a marriage commitment.

Which of the following best describes your view of marriage?

☐ *Marriage should be considered a vow "til death do us part."*
☐ *Marriage should be considered a promise for "as long as love shall last."*

Whether marriage is ultimately based on a decision ("*til death do us part*") or a feeling ("*as long as love shall last*"), it impacts a person's commitment level.

Every marriage is based on either a *Covenant Commitment for Marriage* or a *Contract-Based Relationship*.

What kind of marriage relationship are you wanting to commit to?

☐ *A Covenant Commitment for Marriage*
☐ *A Contract-Based Relationship*

A *Covenant Commitment for Marriage* is the third and final ingredient of the *Foundation for a Lifelong Marriage*.

Take the age of your mate, and subtract it from 77 (the average lifespan for a person). The total will show the estimated length of your lifetime together as husband and wife.

77 - _____ = _____ estimated married years together

How will you keep your Covenant Commitment for Marriage?

Can you think of any circumstances that would cause you to break your Covenant Commitment for Marriage with your mate? If yes, list them below.

On every application for a dissolution, couples must cite a reason for the divorce. The most popular reasons include:

--Irreconcilable differences
--Adultery
--Alcoholism / Drug abuse
--Domestic violence
--Spousal neglect
--Incarceration
--Impotence
--Abandonment
--Sexual abuse
--Infertility

▪ *To the best of your knowledge, do you believe the person you are planning to marry can keep their vows to you? Can you keep your vows to them?*

▪ *List any reservations or concerns you may have in regards to either of you keeping your vows to one another.*

▪ *Write out up to ten promises you will vow to your mate on the wedding day. (This does not need to be poetic or of a certain length.)*

▪ *Do you affirm the three ingredients of the Foundation for a Lifelong Marriage? If not, describe the foundation your marriage will be built upon.*

Couple Time - Discussion Questions

As a couple, discuss *Lay the Foundation for a Lifelong Marriage*. The questions below are to spark conversation and discussion. Capture points of agreement, disagreement, or issues to further discuss below.

What is the foundation for your future marriage? Do you and your mate agree on the foundation?

What differences of opinion do you have about what marriage is?

Do you share a common vision for marriage? Is it God's Four-Fold Vision for Marriage or something else?

Do the two of you define love differently?

How will you demonstrate a Five-Dimensional Love to one another?

Do you both possess a Covenant Commitment for Marriage?

How will you keep your Covenant Commitment for Marriage?

Do you both want a marriage focused on "til death do you part" or "for as long as love shall last?"

What threats exist that could jeopardize your marriage relationship?

DAY SEVEN

Marriage Investor Session Notes

Use this space to capture notes, thoughts, and issues that arise while meeting with your Marriage Investor.

Go Deeper

At **www.FullMarriageExperience.com** you will find lists of helpful books and articles, informative web sites, and practical resources related to topics covered in this section.

- *Research on Marriage and Divorce*
- *Marriage-Related Cultural Issues*
- *Love*
- *Commitment*
- *Covenant*

Section 2
Discover God's Gift to You - Your Mate

What initially attracted you to each other?

Looking beyond physical appearances, usually a distinctive character trait or two sticks out. He liked how *"she spoke her mind"* and he enjoyed her *"spontaneous nature."* She was attracted to his *"strong leadership style"* and how he *"always made her laugh."*

Fast forward after five years of 24/7 married-living and those initial attractive qualities can be a source of irritation.

He thinks *"she has an opinion about everything"* and is *"always late and kind of flaky."* She thinks he is really *"bossy and works too much"* and anytime she brings up serious things, *"he's always cracking jokes."*

No matter how much time a couple spends together, regardless of how much they have in common, despite how well they think they know each other — a husband and wife can get on each other's nerves.

It's almost second nature to realize the differences between oneself and their mate. Appreciating them as God-given characteristics and traits can be a difficult pill to swallow. But mutual respect and unconditional acceptance are necessary for a healthy marriage relationship.

Section two, ***Discover God's Gift to You - Your Mate***, helps couples recognize how similar and how different they really are. From there, couples learn how to take their differences and make them into a strength for their relationship. In addition, they discover how to make their similarities into a greater marriage asset.

> ***In the space provided below, briefly describe your mate as if someone has never met them before.***

DAY ONE | Mega-Different - As God Prescribed

the Bible says

"God said, 'It's not good for the Man to be alone; I'll make him a helper, a companion.' So God formed from the dirt of the ground all the animals of the field and all the birds of the air. He brought them to the Man to see what he would name them. Whatever the Man called each living creature, that was its name. The Man named the cattle, named the birds of the air, named the wild animals; be he didn't find a suitable companion.

God put the Man into a deep sleep. As he slept he removed one of his ribs and replaced it with flesh. God then used the rib that he had taken from the Man to make Woman and presented her to the Man.

The Man said, 'Finally! Bone of my bone, flesh of my flesh! Name her Woman for she was made from Man.' Therefore a man leaves his father and mother and embraces his wife. They become one flesh."
Genesis 2:18-24

worthy quote

"God made woman beautiful and foolish; beautiful, that man might lover her; and foolish, that she might love him."

"Women always worry about the things that men forget; men always worry about the things women remember."

"A woman worries about the future until she gets a husband, while a man never worries about the future until he gets a wife."
-- Anonymous

When God presented the woman to the man, Adam was awestruck by "this creature" God had made for him. She stirred up emotions and feelings in him that no other animal, bird, or fish had.

She was similar and different at the same time. While she was human like Adam, she had distinct physical characteristics unlike Adam's. While they communicated with the same language, they responded to temptation and trials differently.

While only a brief amount of Scripture describes the relationship between Adam and Eve, it can be assumed that the years they spent together were not always heavenly bliss. Over the rest of their lives, Adam and Eve would discover each other's strengths and weaknesses, similarities and differences, and reactions to the good times and the bad.

Today, the growing body of research is uncovering just how different men and women are (and different is an understatement). Men and women are biologically, physiologically, emotionally, and physically different. But distinctive gender characteristics are only the tip of the iceberg to the broad array of differences the two people in marriage possess.

Every human being is a complex makeup of differing personality characteristics, a range of temperament qualities, and a wide variety of character traits. Some are learned, others are naturally produced by our Maker, and others adapt in different environments and seasons of life.

Once a relationship between a man and a woman begins, the differences that initially attracted the couple together can digress into potentially relationship-dividing wedges. This occurs when couples get tunnel vision on their differences. If this slanted focus continues for too long, it can become the reasoning for the *"irreconcilable differences"* citation on their divorce certificate.

Couples must realize that their irreconcilable differences will always exist. Irreconcilable differences exist before, on, and after the wedding day. Viewing one's mate as a gift from God is key to making those irreconcilable differences reconcilable.

Embracing one's spouse as a gift from God is necessary to live the *Full Marriage Experience*. Your *"gift from God"* (your mate) has quirks, idiosyncrasies, and personality differences. So does their *"gift from God"* (you). Attempting to change one's mate is futile, as many broken marriages can testify. Unconditionally accepting one's mate is the secret ingredient in marriages that last.

> *In the space provided, list up to five of <u>your own</u> quirks, idiosyncrasies, or personality differences that could impact your relationship with your mate.*

Charting Your Similarities & Differences

You and your mate will discover how much you have in common and how different you are through the charts on the following pages. Discovering the distinctive differences early in the relationship will not eliminate future struggles triggered by these potential stress points. This process can produce a healthy perspective to help couples understand and appreciate those personal differences. Affirming one another's unique makeup is a marriage strength.

The charts on the following pages focus on four different components that make up every person—interests, personality and temperament, life history, and deeply held personal rules for life.

worthy quote

"You are who you are"

You are who you are for a reason. You're part of an intricate plan. You're a precious and perfect unique design, called God's special woman or man.

You look like you look for a reason. Our God made no mistake. He knit you together within the womb, you're just what he wanted to make.

The parents you had were the ones he chose, And no matter how you may feel, they were custom-designed with God's plan in mind, And they bear the Master's seal.

No, that trauma you faced was not easy. And God wept that it hurt you so; but it was allowed to shape your heart so that into his likeness you'd grow.

You are who you are for a reason, you've been formed by the Master's rod. You are who you are, beloved, because there is a God.
-- Russell Kelfer, poet

Chart 1: Noting the Favorites (pg. 26)
The first chart is designed to discover interests, personal preferences, and the more trivial areas of life.

Chart 2: Unraveling the Hard Wiring (pgs. 28 & 29)
The second chart is two pages. It focuses on the natural tendencies, temperaments, and general make up of different personality types. Wiring can be impacted by family background and by environment. Some wiring is learned, while other wiring is innate.

Chart 3: Traveling the Life Path Journeyed (pg. 31)
The third chart focuses on a person's life path—past and present life experiences that have contributed to making them who they are today. The life lessons learned from these experiences are nearly impossible to unlearn. This chart targets the most influential periods of a person's life journey up to this point in time.

Chart 4: Uncovering the Core Values (pg. 33)
The final chart deals with some of the most basic and important questions of life. These are the foundational pieces for almost every decision a person makes, the personal life rules they live by, and the core values they possess.

All four charts are structured in the same way.

The first column has a word, phrase or question. Write your responses in the second and fourth columns with the headings, "ME on ME", and "ME on MATE." The first response column (ME on ME) is how you describe yourself. The third column (ME on MATE) is how you describe your mate.

During the *Couple Time - Discussion Questions*, share your responses. Write your mate's responses in the blank columns "MATE on ME" to capture how your mate describes you and "MATE on MATE" how your mate describes themself.

worthy quote

"The only time a woman can really succeed in changing a man is when he is a baby."
-- Natalie Wood, actress

Chart 1: Noting the Favorites

	ME on ME	MATE on ME	ME on MATE	MATE on MATE
Food				
Beverage				
Type of Food				
Restaurant				
Singer/Group				
Type of Music				
Book				
Author				
Magazine				
Radio Station				
Movie				
TV Show				
Website				
Color				
School Subject				
Vacation Spot				
Hobby				
Holiday				
Automobile				

■ ***Do you and your mate share more similar or more different interests?***

■ ***Overall, do you feel the individual interests of you and your mate draw you closer together, divide you further apart, or have no effect on your relationship? Why?***

Your interests are not so much a "make-or-break" area in a relationship as it is an intriguing beginning point to the deeper areas of life.

Unraveling the Hard Wiring

DAY THREE

On the line below, write your full name

_____

On the line below, write your full name
(with your other hand).

_____

More than likely the writing on the top line looks better than the writing on the bottom line. That is because you have a tendency to write with one hand over the other. Notice the first set of directions did not indicate which hand to write with. People tend to write with their most naturally comfortable hand.

Every person on the planet has a different set of preferences of how they do things, the process by which they think, and how they process information. These preferences are as natural as writing with one's strong hand. They are God-given, natural, familiar, and valid.

When a couple marries, misunderstanding one another's natural preferences can be a source of frustration: *"Why does he do that?" "Why does she say things like that?" "Why doesn't he do it like this?" "Why doesn't she loosen up and relax?"*

Chart 2: Unraveling the Hard Wiring diffuses the future (or current) frustration by shedding light on the wiring of one's mate.

Respond to each description with the first answer that comes to mind. Avoid over analyzing the statement. Because work life is highly structured and causes people to adjust their natural tendencies, when answering, think of the person outside of the work environment. Good luck and happy discovery!

"What counts in making a happy marriage is not so much how compatible you are, but how you deal with incompatibility."
-- Leo Tolstoy, *author of War and Peace*

take a note

Hard Wiring: Every person on the planet has a different set of preferences of how they do things, the process by which they think, and how they process information.

"...married life brings to the surface your worst attributes: irritability and impatience, defensiveness and self-justification, insensitivity and manipulativeness, and, above all, selfishness. Marriage does not create these traits in us; it exposes them.

The point, however, is not simply to learn to recognize faults. A good marriage teaches what it means to forgive, to let go of grievances, to yield when appropriate, to compromise and work together toward a common goal, to put the interests of another above your own. It is because these things do not come naturally that marriage is so good for so many of us."
-- William J. Bennett, *author of The Book of Virtues*

Chart 2: Unraveling the Hard Wiring

	ME on ME	MATE on ME	ME on MATE	MATE on MATE
Friendships *Numerous acquaintances or handful of good friends?*				
Trust Level *Trust others easily or cautious to trust others?*				
Group Settings *Outspoken or reserved to speak?*				
Energy Recharger *By being with others or being alone?*				
Spending Time *People person or prefer independence?*				
Arrival Time *Punctual or consistently late?*				
Conversations *Tend to be a talker or listener?*				
Learning Style *Auditory, visual, or hands-on learner?*				
Learning *Attracted to details or prefer generalities?*				
Incentive to Act *Prone to act with goals, encouragement, or guilt?*				
Motivation *Rather have grand vision or step-by-step details?*				
Decision Making *Tend to make decisions with the head or the heart?*				
Processing Info *More comfortable with facts or ideas?*				
Relaxation *Results from sleeping, hobbies, physical activities, or being a homebody?*				

Chart 2: Unraveling the Hard Wiring

	ME on ME	MATE on ME	ME on MATE	MATE on MATE
Daily Routine *Similiar patterns or continually need change?*				
Planning *Need a detailed plan or rather improvise?*				
Surroundings *Prefer structure or flexibility?*				
Attaining Goals *Process-oriented or outcome-oriented?*				
In Stressful Times *Tend to be calm or excitable?*				
Anger Gage *Easily angered, slow to anger or repress anger?*				
Reliability *Trustworthy or undependable?*				
Anger Expression *Vent, internalize, become physical, or talk through?*				
Leadership Style *Visionary, manage people, manage details, follower?*				
Assertiveness *Tend to be more bold or more timid?*				
Flexibility *Able to go with the flow or tend to be more rigid?*				
Self-Confidence *Self assured, critical of self, or insecure?*				
View of Life *Optimistic, idealistic, realistic, or pessimistic?*				
Daytime Preference *Morning person or night owl?*				

■ *List three of the strongest similarities in Hard Wiring you and your mate have (based only on your answers).*

■ *How can these similarities be a strength in your relationship? How can the similarities be detrimental to your relationship?*

■ *List three of the strongest differences in Hard Wiring you and your mate have (based only on your answers).*

■ *How can these differences be a strength in your relationship? How can the differences be detrimental in your relationship?*

DAY FOUR — Traveling the Life Path Journeyed

Life is a journey. When a person steps from the path of singleness to the pathway of matrimony, they are continuing on their personal journey of life while beginning a new journey called marriage. Pieces of a person's past can and will impact the couple's day-to-day married life.

Experiences shape and mold people. Knowing the significant people in a person's life, significant events in their life (positive and negative), how they were raised, and where they grew up can give greater insight into who a person is and why they do the things they do. Charting one's **Life Path** forces contemplation over one's past and provides great insight into who they are today, and what they may be tomorrow.

Traveling with one's mate on their *Life Path* (by sharing stories and experiences) enables couples to develop a deepened level of intimacy, greater appreciation for one another, and better understanding of each other.

Chart 3: Traveling the Life Path Journeyed

	ME on ME	MATE on ME	ME on MATE	MATE on MATE
Significant People *List three people (other than fiancé) who have had the greatest impact on you.*	1. 2. 3.	1. 2. 3.	1. 2. 3.	1. 2. 3.
Positive Events *List three positive events that have been significant in your life.*	1. 2. 3.	1. 2. 3.	1. 2. 3.	1. 2. 3.
Negative Events *List three negative events that have been significant in your life.*	1. 2. 3.	1. 2. 3.	1. 2. 3.	1. 2. 3.
Home Life *Raised in the same home all your life, moved within state, moved regularly or frequently?*				
Parents' Marital Status *Raised with biological parents married, divorced, remarried, unmarried, or other?*				
Birth Order *Oldest, youngest, in the middle? List number of siblings and step siblings.*				
Family Relationship *Quality of entire family relationship great, good, average, or poor?*				
Economic Upbringing *Raised majority of life at poverty level, lower, middle, or upper class?*				
Geographic Setting *Raised in a rural, urban, or suburban setting?*				

Each bride and groom marries a foreigner. Everyone comes from: a different land (home raised in), a different people group (families they were raised with), a different culture (customs and traditions their family held), with a different language (ways their family interacted).

Though couples may have the same skin color, speak the same languages, or been raised in the same county - individually, they are completely different.

"God, my shepherd! I don't need a thing. You have bedded me down in lush meadows, you find me quiet pools to drink from. True to your word, you let me catch my breath and send me in the right direction. Even when the way goes through Death Valley, I'm not afraid when you walk at my side. Your trusty shepherd's crook makes me feel secure."
Psalm 23:1-4

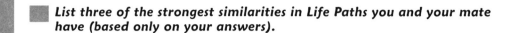

■ ***List three of the strongest similarities in Life Paths you and your mate have (based only on your answers).***

■ ***How can these similarities be a strength in your relationship? How can these similarities be detrimental to your relationship?***

■ ***List three of the strongest differences in Life Paths you and your mate have (based only on your answers).***

■ ***How can these differences be a strength in your relationship? How can these differences be detrimental to your relationship?***

DAY FIVE   Uncovering the Core Values

Core Values: The foundational core of a person's being and the reasoning for almost every decision a person makes, the motivation for why they do what they do, and the basis for who they are.

There are no deeper and more basic questions than *"Why am I here," "What is the purpose of life,"* and *"Is there a God?"* While these questions can be compartmentalized for discussion in a philosophy class, a theology course, or a religious setting, core values impact virtually everything a person does, says, thinks, and desires.

Core Values can be the source of great harmony or great division in a marriage. *Where does a couple turn in the midst of tragedy? What values and morals will be passed down to future family generations? What will their basis be for perceiving right and wrong?*

By uncovering each person's *Core Values*, couples perch themselves from a unique vantage point. They are peering into the foundational core of a person's existence. They expose the reasoning for almost every decision a person makes, the motivation for why they do what they do, and the basis for who they are.

Chart 4: Uncovering the Core Values

	ME on ME	MATE on ME	ME on MATE	MATE on MATE
Meaning of Life *What is the ultimate meaning of life?*				
Worldview *What is the basis for most every decision you make? (feel good, have fun, help others, please God, etc.)*				
Source for Morals *Where do the personal morals you live by come from? (public opinion, parents, faith, peers, religious book, etc.)*				
Moral Basis *How is good and evil, right and wrong determined in your life?*				
Central Priority *What is the number one thing that motivates you for living your life the way you do?*				
Values Priority *Do you place more importance on inward character qualities or outward behavior?*				
Purpose of Life *What is a person's purpose and reason for living?*				
Political Leaning *Currently liberal, conservative, moderate, socialist, or other? List any political affiliation.*				
Causes in Life *List social, political, religious, and other efforts and causes you have participated in.*				

List three of the strongest similarities in Core Values you and your mate have (based only on your answers).

How can the similar Core Values be a strength in your relationship? How can they be detrimental to your relationship?

List three of the strongest differences in Core Values you and your mate have (based only on your answers)?

How can the different Core Values be a strength in your relationship? How can they be detrimental to your relationship?

Assess the Similarities & Differences

You have now identified the similarities and differences in interests, personality and temperament, life history, and personal rules for life.

Can you appreciate and affirm your mate's differences throughout a lifetime together? List any reservations you may have.

How will you affirm the differences between you and your mate?

Can your mate appreciate and affirm your differences throughout a lifetime together? List any reservations.

How can your mate affirm you and the differences you possess?

Do you believe your mate has strengths to fill your weaknesses and differences to fill your gaps? List three strengths/differences they have that you need.

Do you believe you have strengths to fill your mate's weaknesses and differences to fill their gaps? List three strengths/differences you have that they need.

DAY SIX | Couple Time - Discussion Questions

As a couple, compare your responses from all four charts in **Discover God's Gift to You - Your Mate.** Remember to write down your mate's responses in the remaining columns. Have fun learning how different and how similar you two really are.

The questions and statements below are meant to spark further conversation and discussion. Capture points of agreement, disagreement, or issues for further discussion.

Record how many similar Favorite Things you and your mate possess (out of 19).

What different interests do you have from your mate?

How will your personal interests affect your married life?

Record how many similar Hard Wiring characteristics you and your mate possess (out of 28).

Are you and your mate more similar or different in Hard Wiring? List any concerns.

Record how many similar Life Path experiences you and your mate possess (out of 9).

Share with one another additional details pertaining to the Life Path you have journeyed to this point.

Record how many similar Core Values you and your mate share (out of 9).

Do you and your mate share more or fewer Core Values? List any concerns.

Overall, what compromises are the two of you willing to make to appreciate the differences each of you possess?

Marriage Investor Session Notes

DAY SEVEN

Use this space to capture notes, thoughts, and issues that arise while meeting with your Marriage Investor.

Go Deeper

At **www.FullMarriageExperience.com** you will find lists of helpful books and articles, informative web sites, and practical resources related to topics covered in this section.

- *Personality Differences*
- *Gender Differences*
- *Temperament Differences*

Section 3

Survive a Positive Identity Change

"You are now husband and wife!"

Those six words establish a new identity. Actually, three new identities form—a couple, a husband, and a wife.

By exchanging their vows and committing themselves to one another, the groom and bride begin new roles *(husband or wife)*, share a new name *(Mr. and Mrs. Smith)*, and start a new relationship *(marriage)*. These new identities come with new functions and responsibilities that alter the couple's relationship and their families.

Some couples believe they are ready for the identity change. They know marriage will usher them into a new existence, and a new life begins after the wedding day. Other couples are unprepared for the identity change and may find themselves in the middle of an identity crisis before their first anniversary.

The level of readiness depends on the choices a couple makes. Will the couple proactively prepare for their new identity, or will they let the chips fall where they may? Where will they turn for direction and guidance to help them transition into their new identities—popular culture, church, other people, the Bible, television, the latest relationship expert?

Understanding the identity changes in marriage does not have to be a guessing game. Prospective husbands and wives can look to the Author of Marriage to guide them into their new roles, functions, and responsibilities.

This section, **Survive a Positive Identity Change**, exposes couples to issues related to their new identities, roles, and functions as husband, wife, and married couple. Replacing the guesswork with insight, couples can step into their new life together with confidence and understanding. By discovering their new identities, couples can survive the positive identity change, and ultimately live the *Full Marriage Experience*.

▨ *Describe how you think your roles in your relationship will change after the wedding day.*

DAY ONE

Step Out of One Family & Into Another

The majority of a person's life has been under the care, authority, and trust of their parents. The family in which someone was raised shapes that person's views, beliefs, and attitudes about relationships.

What one thinks it means to be a husband, a wife, and a married couple is heavily shaped by their home life. The marriage, ex-marriage, or non-marriage of their parents influences a person's ideas about and vision for the marriage roles. "Family of Origin" issues also affect perceptions and beliefs about family life and parenting.

marriage factoid

In 2002, the living arrangements of children under 18 were as follows:

-- 69% with two parents
--23% with their mother
-- 5% with their father
-- 4% with no parents

-- *U.S. Census Bureau*

Mark all that describe your father's <u>role as a husband</u> (substitute step father if necessary).

- ☐ Endearing husband
- ☐ Missing-in-action partner
- ☐ Well-balanced leader
- ☐ Walked-over spouse
- ☐ Family overseer
- ☐ Dominating husband
- ☐ Emotionally-disengaged mate
- ☐ Mom's best friend
- ☐ Hard-working provider
- ☐ Other _____

Mark all that describe your mother's <u>role as a wife</u> (substitute step mother if necessary).

- ☐ Loving wife
- ☐ Non-existent in family life
- ☐ Over-involved busybody
- ☐ Control freak
- ☐ Glue-of-the-family
- ☐ Nagging wife
- ☐ Passive partner
- ☐ Dad's best friend
- ☐ Sole/dual provider
- ☐ Other _____

How does your parents' modeling of being a husband and wife impact your view of the roles of husband and wife?

In your opinion, is the marriage of your parents a model worth following, a model worth forgetting, or somewhere in between? Why?

To fully step into the marriage relationship, the man and woman must step out of their parents' home, authority, and care. The Scriptural concept of **Leaving** is the first in a two-step process to enter marriage.

While living with one's parents until the wedding day is not as common as it once was, the concept of *Leaving* is more necessary than people may think. *Leaving* does not mean the end of the parent-child relationship. That special bond will still remain after the wedding day. Marriage simply redefines it. To *Leave* means to withdraw from the emotional security, financial dependence, and physical attachments from one's parents.

The Scriptural concept of **Cleaving** is the second step to enter marriage. When a person withdraws from their parents' broad array of support, they must go to someone else who will provide it. Depositing the emotional security, financial dependence, and physical attachments to one's spouse makes the *Leaving and Cleaving* process complete.

For the best interest of everyone, the relational withdrawal and deposit *(Leaving and Cleaving)* should occur as close to the actual wedding day as possible. Attempting to do it well before the wedding or well after the wedding can complicate the couple's relationship and disrupt the extended family relationships. The transition on the wedding day is one of the many spectacular mysteries of marriage.

Why should someone getting married Leave their parents?

List potential pitfalls for couples who do not Leave their parents.

Are you prepared to Leave and Cleave? Is your mate ready to Leave and Cleave? What issues remain?

Do you believe your parents understand the concept and see the necessity in your Leaving them and Cleaving to your spouse?
☐ yes   ☐ no

Do you believe your mate's parents understand the concept and see the necessity in your mate Leaving them and Cleaving to you?
☐ yes   ☐ no

the Bible says

"...'Haven't you read in your Bible that the Creator originally made man and woman for each other, male and female? And because of this, a man leaves father and mother and is firmly bonded to his wife, becoming one flesh—no longer two bodies but one. Because God created this organic union of the two sexes, no one should desecrate his art by cutting them apart.'"
Matthew 19:4-6

worthy quote

"Be tolerant of the human race. Your whole family belongs to it — and some of your spouse's family does too."
-- Unknown

DAY TWO

Three Types of Couple Identities

The first change marked by the wedding is the identity of the couple. Never again will people view the man and woman the same. Their lives have merged and their family trees have forever grafted together. All couples experience the transition to married life; their perspective of what the relationship is supposed to look like affects their **Couple Identity.** Out of three types of *Couple Identities*, two are the polar opposite extremes, and one is in the balance.

-- *OVERLY DEPENDENT COUPLE*

This couple reflects a one-way relationship where one person dominates and the other compromises. One of the parties has an over-reliance on the other for a sense of self-worth and is overly-dependent on the other to feel adequate. They subject their thoughts, abilities, and existence fully to the authority and approval of the other. An *Overly Dependent Couple* is never satisfied, always dysfunctional, and, in too many cases, abusive.

-- *OVERLY INDEPENDENT COUPLE*

This couple reflects a two-way relationship where the separate lives of the man and woman may intersect at various times, but can often go in separate directions. Over time, this type of couple can find themselves living as married-singles. The parties decidedly choose not to rely too heavily on each other. The *Overly Independent Couples* tends to take steps and make decisions to avoid infringing on each others' independence.

The idea of a "50/50 relationship" typifies this couple. While the 50/50 approach may be helpful for some business partnerships, it can be detrimental in intimate relationships. *Overly Independent Couples* may be satisfied with the relationship for awhile, but the moment they feel they are giving more than the other (51% or more)—feelings of betrayal and bitterness replace joy and happiness.

-- *INTERDEPENDENT COUPLE*

This couple reflects a relationship of mutuality. Together, they mutually decide to depend on one another, be influenced by one another, and rely on one another. The *Interdependent Couple* is the couple identity reflected throughout the Christian Scriptures.

Interdependent Couples must have healthy relationships. They need to know how to communicate, resolve conflict, and make sacrifices. By sharing a common vision for marriage, striving for common goals, and living for a common purpose—the *Interdependent Couple* sets in motion a cycle of mutual care.

Life is unpredictable. It has its challenges and triumphs. As a team, the *Interdependent Couple* strives together on the pathway to a successful, life-long marriage journey, that leads to the *Full Marriage Experience*.

"Any woman who still thinks marriage is a fifty-fifty proposition is only proving that she doesn't understand either men or percentages."
-- Rose Kennedy, mother of John F. Kennedy

"A good marriage is one which allows for change and growth in the individuals and in the way they express their love."
-- Pearl S Buck, Nobel Prize winning author

■ *Which Couple Identity reflects your pre-marriage relationship? What evidence do you have for this claim?*

■ *Which Couple Identity reflects your desire for your marriage relationship? Why?*

■ *In the margin are married couples featured on television's most popular shows. List three of the couples whose on-screen relationships you most admire and three you do not.*

Roles - A Partnership Made in Heaven

DAY THREE

In spite of a high esteem for weddings and marriage, there is great confusion surrounding the roles and functions of a husband and wife. There are two prevailing but opposing views on the spousal roles.

One side of the spectrum embraces a set of rules, duties, and expectations for the husband and wife based on specific gender roles. It is based loosely on some Scripture passages, and largely on an aged ideology of male-superiority/female-inferiority. Family relationships are patriarchal and authoritarian. While the media stereotypes this as the norm in all religious marriages and families, it is a point of view that is not widely accepted.

The other side of the spectrum disregards the distinctive qualities and gender characteristics within husbands and wives. It attempts to neutralize the God-given differences between a man and a woman and create a unisex role in marriage. One person is no different than the other. The husband and wife are simply titles for each gender in the marriage, and nothing more. In an attempt to fill the cultural confusion gap on roles with an inoffensive ideal, this viewpoint suggests a husband and wife bring nothing of unique importance to the marriage relationship.

Both viewpoints fall short of giving meaningful purpose for both the husband and the wife. Authoritarian and unisex beliefs miss the mark of God's ideal for the marriage relationship.

So what did God have in mind with the spousal roles?

"...marriage rests on the basic complementarity of man and woman, the complementarity that drives two independent people to become, in the biblical phrase, 'one flesh.' And this complementarity is itself based on fundamental differences between men and women that are physical and emotional, psychological and sexual. Indeed, it is these very differences —these complementary differences—that help men and women achieve, in marriage, unity and interdependence, completeness and fulfillment."
-- William J. Bennett, *author of Our Sacred Honor*

the Bible says

"In a marriage relationship, there is authority from Christ to husband, and from husband to wife. The authority of Christ is the authority of God ... Don't by the way, read too much into the differences here between men and women. Neither man nor woman can go it alone or claim priority. Man was created first, as a beautiful shining reflection of God—that is true. But the head on a woman's body clearly outshines in beauty the head of her 'head,' her husband. The first woman came from man, true—but ever since then, every man comes from a woman! And since virtually everything comes from God anyway, let's quit going through these 'who's first' routines."
I Corinthians 11:3; 11-12

the Bible says

"Out of respect for Christ, be courteously reverent to one another. Wives, understand and support your husbands in ways that show support for Christ. The husband provides leadership to his wife the way Christ does to his church, not by domineering but by cherishing. So just as the church submits to Christ as he exercises such leadership, wives should likewise submit to their husbands."
Ephesians 5:21-24

Marriage is a partnership with primary roles and distinct functions. God's perspective of the man and woman are equal in regard, equal in value, and equal in worth.

As a husband and wife, they are called to equally important, yet different roles and functions. God's calling to the husband and wife in the marriage roles and responsibilities are a bit different, but not because one is inferior or less important to the marriage. Both the husband and wife are necessary to experience all God intended in marriage.

God set up the marriage roles based on interdependence and mutual respect. Like a team working together, a husband and wife fill unique functions in the relationship that maximize their talents and gifts. Their different roles increase the potential for the couple to reach a common good — to bring out the best in the other, and ultimately live the *Full Marriage Experience.*

God's primary role for a husband is to be a **Servant Leader.**

God designed an order in marriage for the purpose of harmony, unity, and fulfillment in the relationship. The husband is not a CEO, master, or his wife's boss. As a *Servant Leader*, he constantly looks out for her best interest in all situations. He is to be willing to lay down his life for her. Husbands are called to follow the model of Jesus Christ, who displayed servant leadership by being servant-minded, selfless in His actions, and sacrificial in His leadership. He did not flaunt or misuse His leadership. He did all He could to bring out the best in others.

> -- *Seeing the stress Sandy's new job was putting on her, Jim began cooking and grocery shopping so she could relax after work.*

> -- *Knowing that attending church as a couple was important to Patty, Les gave up his late Saturday poker nights so he could join her on Sunday mornings.*

God's primary role for a wife is to be a **Supportive Counterpart.**

A wife who demonstrates respect, trust, and honor towards her husband will receive love and care in return. While God has established the husband as the "head" in the marriage, the wife adapts to his leadership except in cases where he is directing her to sin against God, or she is in jeopardy of harm.

As a *Supportive Counterpart* she provides insights, perspective and input as an assistant coach provides to a head coach. With both the husband and wife following God and being accountable to Him, they stand poised to experience the fullness of all God has in store for them, individually and as a couple.

> -- *Though she didn't fully comprehend all the details of the plans, Kelly trusted William had the best interest of their family in mind and would make a wise decision.*

> -- *The investment ideas seemed solid to both of them at the time, but after they lost their money, Michelle chose not to heap blame on top of James.*

In their primary roles, the husband seems to oversee the macro-level (more global) issues of the relationship, while the wife seems to oversee the micro-level (more local) issues.

Both are needed to ensure each is contributing to the wholistic well-being of their marriage and family. Neither can adequately assume both levels of oversight. The husband and the wife are necessary and specially designed to successfully live out what God has called them to live out.

What do you feel will be your biggest challenge to living out the spousal role God called you to live out?

What do you think will be the biggest challenge for your mate to live out the spousal role God has called them to live out?

a closer look

The term submission is greatly misunderstood today. Cultural elites describe it as demeaning, patriarchal, and an attempt to put women in a subservient role. Nothing could be further from the truth! Submission means to relinquish one's rights for the better good or the cause of others. In marriage, both the husband and the wife are looking out for each other's best interest as each looks to God for direction and accountability. As husband and wife strive to help the other, there is no room for either to take advantage of the other.

Husband & Wife - Divinely Designed Functions   DAY FOUR

In addition to the passages referring to the primary roles of a husband and wife, other Scriptures provide greater insights on the functions of the spouses.

Throughout Scripture, God calls people by specific name or title to be sure the right people heard an important message. Scripture passages directed at husbands and wives can be seen as God highlighting specific areas for each to focus on, so as a couple they can experience all marriage has to offer them.

The New Testament passages were written as Christianity blossomed in Roman culture. At that time, husbands were supreme masters in their homes and often mistreated and neglected their wives. Treated as property, wives feared their husbands and resented their power over their lives. This vicious cycle destroys God's ideals for marriage. The pain compounds as husbands fail to love their wives and wives disrespect their husbands.

New Testament instruction on marriage challenged the patriarchal mindset of marriage and family life. Christian teachings directed at husbands and wives were radical and counter cultural. This new view and way of living attracted many to explore and embrace Christianity.

Wives were elevated to new levels of equality. Husbands were taught humility and leading with mutual respect. Wives were instructed to respect their husbands. Husbands were instructed to love their wives. Marriages thrived in light of the new, unconventional teachings of Christianity.

The functional instruction for spouses in the 1st Century is as applicable to 21st Century husbands and wives as it was back then.

The specific guidance to husbands and wives could be viewed as God's divine reminders of how they are and are not to act in their **Divinely Designed Functions.**

God's Divine Reminders for Husbands

BE A CHERISHING FRIEND

A husband's mission in life is to intimately know his wife. This means to understand his wife like no one else can, completely appreciating who she is as a person, a woman, and a wife. He is to discover ways to make her feel cherished and respected while tenderly caring for her needs. Essentially, the husband is to treat his wife like royalty—his own personal queen.

- *After dinner, Tim turned the TV off to spend uninterrupted time talking with Tiffany about her day.*

- *Every month, Luke devotes an entire Saturday to do the things Deb likes to do, sleep in, exercise together, shop for antiques, and spend time hanging out.*

BE A WHOLISTIC PROVIDER

Provision goes beyond providing a roof overhead and putting food on the table. A husband provides physically, emotionally, and spiritually for the well-being of his wife and family. He has been called to help instruct his kids about life issues. He is to ensure the environment in the home enriches his wife's whole being — her heart, body, mind, and soul.

- *Anticipating the demands of child-rearing, David and Rachel planned ahead and structured their lifestyle around his sole income so when it was time, she could stay home with the children without financial stress.*

- *Seeing the need for spiritual growth in their lives, Ken makes it a priority to spend time praying with Valerie.*

BE A NOURISHING SUPPORTER

The husband is to do everything he can for his wife so she has every opportunity to mature and flourish in her role as a wife and a woman. He nourishes her soul by giving her every opportunity to excel with continual encouragement to grow into the fullness of who God desires her to be. A husband sets his eyes on empowering their wives to become a better person where it counts the most, on the inside. This is done by nourishing her with a healthy, balanced diet of affirmation rather than a sporadic, fast food style of compliments.

- *After the baby was born, Jeremy quit one of his two softball teams and played less golf so Leanne could do aerobics and join a new mothers class.*

- *Kirk is learning to play tennis so he and Cindy can share a recreational activity together.*

BE AN UNCONDITIONAL LOVER

Unconditional love is a selfless, sacrificial type of love that looks out for another's best interest regardless of what they do. By initiating and modeling this type of love in the marriage, husbands will set the tone for the rest of the household to exhibit selfless attitudes and behaviors. They look out for their wives in every way—physically, emotionally, and spiritually, and put her needs before his own.

- *As Trudy's pregnancy resulted in hormone imbalances, physical changes, and a good amount of time on bed rest, Scott never let a day pass without affirming and supporting her.*

- *Even though Chad was inbetween jobs while Leslie experienced great advancements at work, he arranged a big party to celebrate her promotion.*

Why do you think God is reminding husbands of these Divinely Designed Functions?

the Bible says

"What is clearest to me is the way Christ treats the church. And this provides a good picture of how each husband is to treat his wife, loving himself in loving her..."
Ephesians 5:32-33

"Husbands, go all out in your love for your wives. Don't take advantage of them."
Colossians 3:19

God's Divine Reminders for Wives

BE A RELIABLE HELPMATE

When God made Eve, he designed her as a "helper" for Adam. That does not translate as a maid, cook, or doormat. The wife acts as an ally helping the one in need of help (husband). In so doing, she helps him to reach his full potential, herself to reach her own full potential, and them to reach their full potential. This produces a team-mentality rather than a selfish-mentality in the marriage.

- *April helps the new business venture by handling phone calls and invoices, freeing Steve up to focus on his strengths with clients and new business prospects.*

- *While building their new house, Jeff handled the construction matters while Lisa planned the color schemes, decorations, and accessories.*

BE AN ACTIVE PARTNER

The wife is not to idly wait on the sidelines of life. She is to actively enhance her husband, her family, and her home, therefore enhancing herself. A wife's priority is to look out for her husband and family's best interest. By producing a sense of worth and well-being in the family, she will receive praise, affirmation, and respect from the children and husband. A marriage partnership allows for both the husband and wife to excel in their strengths and complement each other's weaknesses.

the Bible says

"God said, 'It's not good for the Man to be alone; I'll make a helper, a companion.'"
Genesis 2:18

the Bible says

"A good woman is hard to find, and worth far more than diamonds. Her husband trusts her without reserve, and never has reason to regret it. Never spiteful, she treats him generously all her life long ... When she speaks she has something worthwhile to say, and she always says it kindly. She keeps an eye on everyone in her household, and keeps them all busy and productive. Her children respect and bless her; her husband joins in with words of praise: 'Many women have done wonderful things, but you've outclassed them all!'"
Proverbs 31:10-12; 26-29

- *Anne proofs and edits Shaun's post-graduate papers to help him balance work, school, and the training internship.*

- *Julie and Tom talked through all the issues surrounding a potential job promotion that would require them to move across the country.*

BE THE OVERSEER OF THE HOUSEHOLD

Administrating and caring for the household is one of the primary responsibilities of the wife. To manage, run, and guide the affairs of home life takes a special type of person who can balance an array of details, perform multiple acts of laborious service, and at the same time provide for the emotional and instructional needs of their family. God wired women to perform these most vital and important tasks.

- *In the midst of a normal busy life, Kristi manages the family calendar to ensure she and Dan have time to relax, time with the kids, and alone time with each another.*

- *Though a great financial sacrifice, Michael and Deidre decided together that he would take care of providing the family income and she would focus on caring for the kids and home.*

BE A VOCAL CHEERLEADER

People in life are quick to point out faults, weaknesses, and mistakes. The husband does not need more critics in his life. He needs his wife to be supportive and respectful. He needs their home to be a place of refuge. Verbal affirmation goes a long way for a man. It goes even further when it comes from his wife. His wife should be his biggest, loudest, and greatest cheerleader in life.

- *Marena's pride in her husband Jeffrey is evident by the way she talks about him, whether he is present or not.*

- *Margo knows her husband works for a hotheaded manager, so when Doug gets home, she encourages him and builds him up.*

Why do you think God is reminding wives of these Divinely Designed Functions?

How does the relationship benefit if husbands and wives live out these Divinely Designed Functions?

List any functions you would add or delete. Why?

Lay Your Expectations on the Table

*Expectations** are the beliefs people possess about the way things will be or should be in the future (e.g., behaviors, roles, life and death, relationships). Regardless if they are correct or incorrect, right or wrong, realistic or unrealistic-- *Expectations* shape people's perceptions about things and often seep into shaping their view of reality.

Expectations are the beliefs people possess about the way things will be or should be in the future.

If *Expectations* are not met, they can easily lead to feelings of sadness, disappointment, and anger. Over time, this can develop into extreme frustration, disillusionment, and a growing sense of betrayal. To diffuse conflict in a relationship, each person must determine their own *Expectations*, and the *Expectations* of their mate.

Every person walking into marriage has a set of *Expectations* on the roles, responsibilities, identity, and traditions for their relationship. Most times, husbands and wives may be unaware of their viewpoints: they may be unreasonable and unrealistic, or they may be realized and unspoken. As long as *Expectations* remain unaddressed, the health of the relationship and the future of the marriage may be at risk.

Now is the time to determine what *Expectations* exist in the relationship or for the future marriage. *Expectations* expressed and shared prior to the wedding day enable the husband and wife to strive for similar goals within their life together. Take time to think through each of the following questions.

What past family traditions do you expect to carry into your marriage (e.g., mealtime rituals, holidays, vacations, etc.)?

What Expectations are you placing on your mate as they become your husband or wife?

How will you handle it if and when your mate fails to meet your Expectations?

*Used by permission of Christian PREP, Inc. Adapted from the book, *A Lasting Promise* (1998).

Divvying Up the To-Do List

The realities of married life quickly become intertwined with the realities of life. Someone has to take out the garbage. Someone has to cook dinner. And all too often, this *someone* does not find out about this *Expectation* until that *something* has not been done.

To assist in the process of determining who will do what, a list of **Duties and Tasks** is provided below.

The first column (DUTIES & TASKS) lists responsibilities and duties common in married life. The second column (DECIDE) determines the party responsible for the duty and task. The third column (ACT) determines who will have the primary responsibility to carry out that certain duty. Fill in the blank spaces with either HE, SHE, or WE.

Who will primarily be responsible to:

DUTIES & TASKS	DECIDE	ACT
Vacuum the house		
Clean the house		
Maintain exterior of house		
Buy the groceries		
Cook the meals		
Clean the clothes		
Maintain the yard		
Service the vehicles		
Create the budget		
Provide income		
Keep the budget		
Update the checkbook		
Make major purchases		
Plan social schedule		
Care for kids		
Discipline kids		
Teach morals to the kids		
Ensure spiritual growth in family		
Initiate sexual activity		
Coordinate date nights		

How does your list of Duties and Tasks compare to how your parents shared duties and tasks?

Are there any chores that you feel uncomfortable taking responsibility for? Why?

List chores that you definitely want to be responsible for.

Do you have any reservations about your mate sharing responsibility for the Duties and Tasks?

Unmet *Expectations* can devastate a marriage. Whether it's who does what chores, how a spouse will "change" after marriage, or what married life is expected to be like, identifying realistic and unrealistic *Expectations* can be done. With open communication about expectations, couples decrease the chances of being blindsided by strife.

Expectations that don't become reality must not result in resentment; rather, they should result in patience and acceptance. Most couples come to realize that though some of their *Expectations* don't get met, marriage fulfills more in their life than they ever dreamed.

Duties and Tasks. Expectations. Roles and Functions for a husband and wife. The type of **Couple Identity. Leaving and Cleaving.** These are all pieces of the identity change that occur in the transition from singleness to marriage.

Couples who **Survive a Positive Identity Change** are on their way to live the *Full Marriage Experience*.

DAY SIX | Couple Time - Discussion Questions

Take some time to discuss *Survive a Positive Identity Change* with one another. Use the following questions as a guide for your conversation.

- *What changes will you and your mate have to make as you Leave your parents?*

- *What concerns do you and your mate have of Leaving and Cleaving?*

- *List healthy ways to grow a relationship with parents and in-laws after the wedding day.*

- *How can you and your mate honor both sets of parents for their influence in your lives?*

- *How do you expect marriage to change your relationship?*

- *How do you view your role in the relationship changing as you become a husband and wife?*

- *Name couples whose marriage you admire. Share qualities in their relationship you hope to have in your marriage.*

- *Name couples whose marriage you don't respect. Share the negative attributes of their relationship and how you plan to avoid the attributes in your own relationship.*

- *What will you receive through marriage that you would not receive by remaining single?*

- *What chores did your father and mother perform while you were growing up? Compare with your mate's home life experience of which spouse did what chores. Note the differences.*

Marriage Investor Session Notes

DAY SEVEN

Use this space to capture notes, thoughts, and issues that arise while meeting with your Marriage Investor.

Go Deeper

At **www.FullMarriageExperience.com** you will find lists of helpful books and articles, informative web sites, and practical resources related to topics covered in this section.

- *Family of Origin Issues*
- *Roles in Marriage*
- *Husbands*
- *Wives*
- *Expectations*

Section 4

Fight With Your Mate & Please God Too

Relationships would be free of conflict if it weren't for people. But they wouldn't be as meaningful if they were entirely problem-free. A marriage without conflict means one of the people is not necessary in the relationship.

The most common cause for marital strife is rooted in communication breakdown. A couple's inability to resolve conflict is an inability to deal with their differences. For some couples, to talk about problems is to admit that their relationship is flawed.

Marriage blends two individuals with different personality types, different upbringings, and different sets of traditions who choose to spend one lifetime together.

Combine this with the fact that the husband and wife each possess a pair of ears to hear with, a set of lips to speak with, and a brain to process information with; inevitably sparks will fly between a husband and wife. If they can learn to keep those sparks from turning into a fireworks display, they will live the *Full Marriage Experience*.

This section, **Fight With Your Mate & Please God Too** helps couples identify destructive patterns most people use to handle conflict. Couples will also learn how to deal with problems before they happen, and when they do, how to successfully talk it through. Any couple who masters these skills will virtually divorce-proof their marriage.

■ *How do you react to conflict in the workplace or with friends?*

■ *What is your common pattern to resolve conflict with others?*

DAY ONE

Four Fighting Games People Play

marriage factoid

"...a variety of studies suggest that the seeds of marital distress and divorce are there for many couples when they say, 'I do.'"

-- Facts About Marital Distress and Divorce

the Bible says

"Where do you think all these appalling wars and quarrels come from? Do you think they just happen? Think again. They come about because you want your own way, and fight for it deep inside yourselves. You lust for what you don't have and are willing to kill to get it. You want what isn't yours an will risk violence to get your hands on it. You wouldn't think of just asking God for it, would you? And why not? Because you know you'd be asking for what you have no right to. You're spoiled children, each wanting your own way."
James 4:1-3

take a note

Verbal Tug-of-War: Anchoring themselves on opposing sides, partners negatively respond toward one another in a verbal give-and-tug match causing the conversation to escalate.

the Bible says

"Rash language cuts and maims, but there is healing in the words of the wise."
Proverbs 12:18

"Answering before listening is both stupid and rude."
Proverbs 18:13

Every couple will experience times of disagreement, misunderstanding, miscommunication, and a battle of the wills in their relationship. How a couple deals with the conflict is called a **Fighting Game**. Regardless of how "in love" a couple feels, how dignified their backgrounds are, or how important their status in life is, most every couple tends to play one or more of four *Fighting Games**.

The *Fighting Games* are **Verbal Tug-of-War, Put Down Tag, Conspiracy Poker, and Conflict Hide-and-Go-Seek.**

While the *Fighting Games* are different in their expression, they have the same root cause—a couple's inability to resolve conflict.

The first *Fighting Game* is called **Verbal Tug-of-War**. Anchoring themselves on opposing sides, partners negatively respond toward one another in a verbal give-and-take match causing the conversation to escalate.

The example of Ian and Irene Intensity shows a *Verbal Tug-of-War*.

Ian: "Is it too much to ask for you to put away your makeup when you're done? It really clutters up the bathroom when I'm trying to get ready."
Irene: "Oh, and you never forget to put things away?"
Ian: "As a matter of fact, I always put everything back in its proper spot. Unlike you who simply leaves everything everywhere for everybody to deal with."
Irene: "Oh, I didn't realize I lived under the same roof as Mr. Perfect. You are such a neat-freak! It's like being married to my dad the way you always correct me."
Ian: "I am getting so sick of your sloppiness and defensiveness. I don't even know why I put up with it anymore."
Irene: "Maybe you shouldn't stay. The area around the door seems to be clutter-free. Now is your opportunity to leave."

The *Verbal Tug-of-War* displays how conflict can expand from a trivial comment on a toothpaste cap into a marriage-threatening situation. Most bouts of *Verbal Tug-of-War* don't escalate to this level of intensity, but they have a common ingredient—a cycle of exchanging negative comments for negative comments.

■ *List ways the Verbal Tug-of-War can damage a relationship.*

The second *Fighting Game* is **Put Down Tag**. Possessing the self-appointed responsibility of "being It," a partner directly or indirectly puts down the other partner's character, abilities, appearance, ideas, thoughts, or feelings.

Peter and Priscilla Putdown demonstrate *Put Down Tag*.

*Used by permission of Christian PREP, Inc. Adapted from the book, *A Lasting Promise* (1998).

Priscilla: *"The therapist's office called today. You missed your appointment... again! They are charging us for a full visit."*
Peter: *"Oh, I forgot. Sorry."*
Priscilla: *"Did you forget, or are you avoiding seeing the counselor? Don't you want to get better? You are so irresponsible."*
Peter: *"I'm soooooo sorry. Should I remind you of your lack of ability in holding down a job longer than six months? Do we need to rehash who burned the Thanksgiving turkey last year and the year before that? Who is the one that forgot to pick up Peter Jr. from the day care last year?"*
Priscilla: *"At least I am not a TV couch potato like you!"*
Peter: *"You are such a nag."*

Put Down Tag can be caustic or subtle. Rather than focusing on the real issue, the focus is placed on the person in the form of a put down. Priscilla may have valid concerns about Peter's emotional health. But rather than expressing her fears, she launches into him with accusations.

List ways Put Down Tag can damage a relationship.

"Fools have short fuses and explode all too quickly; the prudent quietly shrug off insults."
Proverbs 12:16

The third *Fighting Game* is **Conspiracy Poker**. Creating their own house rules, one partner creates a conspiracy in their mind about the motives, thoughts, and actions of their mate. Instead of confronting their partner by "laying down their cards," they continue to "deal new hands" that support their own internalized suspicions and hunches.

Sam and Sally Skeptical showcase *Conspiracy Poker*.

Sally: *"When do you want to watch the kids so I can register at the college?"*
Sam: *"After balancing the check book and setting up the new budget, I am wondering if we can really afford it this year."*
Sally: *"What? Are you afraid I'm going to fall for some young freshman, or maybe my professor?"*
Sam: *"Stop it. I would love for you to start up this fall. I just don't see how we can afford the tuition with how tight things have been this year. Plus we have Shawn's braces, Stephanie's new car, and Stacy's tutor."*
Sally: *"Just admit it, you don't want me to have my own life."*
Sam: *"There's nothing to admit. I look forward to seeing you go to school. I look forward to seeing you cram for tests. I look forward to seeing you graduate. I just think we need to wait a year is all."*
Sally: *"Yeah, right!"*

Sally put Sam in a situation that he could not penetrate through. No matter how many ways he rephrased his thoughts, she saw it her way. *Conspiracy Poker* can be displayed in "mind reading," assuming one knows the thoughts and motivation behind a person's actions. Often, people will build the case in their mind so slanted, it confirms their suspicions. Unfortunately, this leads to a sense of hopelessness for the partner on the other side of this *Fighting Game*.

Conspiracy Poker: Creating their own house rules, one partner creates a conspiracy in their mind about the motives, thoughts, and actions of their mate. Instead of confronting their partner by "laying down their cards," they continue to "deal new hands" that support their own internalized suspicions and hunches.

Put Down Tag: Possessing the self-appointed responsibility of "being It," a partner directly or indirectly puts down the other partner's character, abilities, appearance, ideas, thoughts, or feelings.

List ways Conspiracy Poker can damage a relationship.

The final *Fighting Game* is **Conflict Hide-and-Go-Seek**. This game begins when one partner withdraws (hides) from a conversation about conflict, avoids the discussion all together, tends to get quiet during an argument, quickly agrees to prematurely end the conversation, or avoids allowing the discussion to occur at all. This can cause the other partner to pursue (seek) the discussion, the conflict, and the partner.

Harry and Hannah Hidenseek play *Conflict Hide-and-Go-Seek*.

Hannah: *"When are we going to talk about last weekend?"*
Harry: *"I'm working on a project. Can't this wait?"*
Hannah: *"No it can't wait. Every time I bring it up, you dodge the discussion."*
Harry: *"What do you want to talk about anyways? It's over with!"*
Hannah: *"You need to do something about your gambling problem! You can't deny it any longer!"*
Harry: *"This discussion is over. I need some fresh air."*
Hannah: *"The discussion never started. You always run away when I confront you. Don't you dare walk out that door!"*
Harry: *"Later."*

When this *Fighting Game* takes place in a relationship (with one hiding from conflict and the other seeming to seek it) it can lead to great frustration for both parties. The withdrawer can think all the pursuer wants to do is fight, gripe, and complain. The pursuer can think the withdrawer doesn't care about the issue, and, therefore, does not care about them. Over time, as *Conflict Hide-and-Go-Seek* continues, both could tend to withdraw from the relationship.

List ways Conflict Hide-and-Go-Seek can damage a relationship.

All four *Fighting Games* are popular patterns of how couples respond to conflict. Most people play the *Fighting Games* to some degree. Often viewed as natural ways of dealing with issues, the *Fighting Games* will slowly devour the threads of joy and happiness from a marriage relationship and replace them with bitterness and strife. As with all games, there is a winner and a loser. But in the case of these *Fighting Games*, both sides lose regardless of who "wins" the argument.

Which Fighting Game(s) do you and your mate most often play?

Stepping Through the Minefield of Mixed Messages

DAY TWO

People are misunderstood all the time. Misunderstandings have sparked wars, torn apart businesses, and broken up friendships.

A person can talk with someone else, but that doesn't guarantee that the other person has listened to what has been said.

In every conversation, the one speaking has "intent" on the message they are conveying (what they want the other to hear, and how they want the listener to respond). The "impact" of one's words is completely based on how the listener receives the information. This can lead to great difficulty in understanding one another because the message sent is not always the message received.

Because **Mixed Messages** are so commonplace, and occur so often, it is helpful to identify and label them. This can help alleviate unnecessary stress and friction in all relationships.

Here are three main reasons why *Mixed Messages* are so common:

-- *Mind Reading*
-- *Miscommunication*
-- *Negative Ways to Raise Concerns*

Mind Reading* occurs when a partner assumes they know what the other partner is thinking.

Sometimes, *Mind Reading* can be good for a marriage: knowing a gift your spouse would like to receive, knowing they would appreciate help on a project, knowing what makes them feel loved. Other times, however, it can be a source of tremendous frustration.

How can Mind Reading damage a relationship?

How often does Mind Reading occur in your relationship? When does it tend to take place?

To overcome the tendency for *Mind Reading*, the mind reader should concentrate on what they think and feel, not on what they think their partner thinks and feels. It forces mind readers to deal with realities rather than perceptions. General communication and resolving conflict will go a lot smoother.

*Used by permission of Christian PREP, Inc. Adapted from the book, *A Lasting Promise* (1998).

"Ask yourself, 'what difference will this thing we're fighting about make in ten years? In one year? In a month?'"
-- Anonymous

"Marriage is one long conversation, checkered with disputes."
-- Robert Louis Stevenson, *author of Treasure Island*

"So don't get ahead of the Master and jump to conclusions with your judgments before all the evidence is in. When He comes, He will bring out in the open and place in evidence all kinds of things we never even dreamed of — inner motives and purposes and prayers."
I Corinthians 4:5

*Miscommunication** is one of the most basic causes for *Mixed Messages* with people. A variety of reasons create a prime breeding ground for *Miscommunication*.

ENVIRONMENTAL FACTORS: If not contained properly, garbage and waste pollute the environment. In day-to-day life, pollutants impact conversations: conversing in a noisy room, speaking through walls, talking surrounded by distracting activity, communicating on a cell phone or by e-mail. All kinds of pollutants can contribute to *Miscommunication*.

WHAT IS SAID: There are several statements to avoid when talking with other people, especially when conflict arises.

-- **"You never..."** *(do things for me; think of me; etc.)*
This statement is false because it accuses someone of something impossible to prove: that they "never" did/do something.

-- **"You always..."** *(have to be right; go out with your friends, etc.)*
This statement is equally untrue because nobody can "always" do something.

-- **"You are..."** *(so dumb; a control freak; a jerk; etc.)*
This statement will most often result in name calling or a personal attack.

-- **"You said..."** *(we would go out tonight; you wanted that; etc.)*
While the claim may be completely accurate, it is pointless to attempt to force a person to remember something they said if they don't remember saying it.

-- **"You make me feel..."** *(dumb; inadequate; angry; etc.)*
While feelings are always valid, a person cannot make another person feel a certain way; their actions or words can, but they themselves cannot.

-- **Devaluing body language** *(rolling of eyes; crossed arms; etc.)*
Body language is the biggest component of unspoken communication, and can quickly cause conversations to nosedive to new depths of intensity.

HOW IT IS SAID: The tone, the style, and the inflections in one's voice can completely unravel the originally intended message. This occurs for a variety of reasons.

-- **Family of Origin:** How one's parents communicated with each other influences children when later in life, they are in their own marriage relationship.

-- **Differences in Wiring:** Temperaments and wiring play a role: an extrovert compared to an introvert, a wordy person with a verbally concise person, a person highly excitable to stress compared to a person who is calm through stress.

-- **Self-Protection:** People attempt to protect themselves from rejection by couching statements in a non-threatening question: *"Wouldn't you like to...?"* rather than *"I would like to..."*

*Used by permission of Christian PREP, Inc. Adapted from the book, *A Lasting Promise* (1998).

■ **How can Miscommunication impact a relationship?**

■ **What contributes to Miscommunication the most in your relationship (environment, what you say, how you say it)?**

Negative Ways to Raise Concerns is another contributor to *Mixed Messages* between a husband and wife. While the heart of the message may be sincere, how the topic is raised can thrust the conversation in a completely different direction. Here are three popular ways people negatively raise concerns:

-- **Mudslinging**— assassinates the character of the person rather than dealing with the problem itself.
   "You probably forgot to send the phone bill in again, huh?"

-- **Doomsdaying**— assumes the issue is so big and catastrophic that there is no hope of ever overcoming it.
   "We will never be able to afford a house of our own!"

-- **Faultfinding**— assuming it is always the other person's fault. Some problems are due to a sole person, but often problems are the result of both people in the relationship.
   "It's all your fault we are in debt as deep as we are!"

■ **How can Mudslinging, Doomsdaying, and Faultfinding damage a relationship?**

the Bible says

"Carelessly call a brother 'idiot!' and you just might find yourself hauled into court. Thoughtlessly yell 'stupid!' at a sister and you are on the brink of hellfire. The simple moral fact is that words kill."
Matthew 5:22

■ **Do you or your mate Mudsling? Doomsday? Faultfind? Why?**

■ **What can you and your mate do to avoid Mixed Messages?**

DAY THREE

Pathway to Successful Communication

marriage factoid

The following are the three most problematic issues in the first five years of marriage.

1. Balance job & family
2. Frequency of sexual relations
3. Debt brought into marriage

-- Time, Sex and Money: The First Five Years of Marriage

a closer look

STRUCTURE
(Structured Talk Tools)
+
SAFETY
(Safe Talking Game Plan)
+
BOUNDARIES
(A Couple's Peace Plan)
=
AUTHENTIC, GENU-INE, OPEN, EFFECTIVE COMMUNICATION

worthy quote

"A couple's mindset about conflict and how they resolve conflict is the single most significant predictor of whether or not a marriage can thrive."
-- Julie Baumgardner, *marriage advocate*

the Bible says

"Post this at all the intersections, dear friends: Lead with your ears, follow up with your tongue, and let anger straggle along in the rear. God's righteousness doesn't grow from human anger."
James 1:19-20

The previous pages have revealed the negative and ineffective ways people often deal with problems. It is time to concentrate on effective and constructive ways to handle conflict that will build up the relationship and ensure couples live the *Full Marriage Experience.*

Because problems are a part of life, all couples will encounter them throughout their lifetime journey together. Many people have the tendency to handle problems too quickly. While this technique for swift problem solving can be a strength in the workplace, it will result in relational friction in the marriage. Quick solutions are not lasting solutions. rapid problem solving tends to gloss over the real issues and rob couples of the opportunity to work through the issue as a team.

Regardless of the circumstances, situation, or trial, the *Pathway to Successful Communication* has three necessary ingredients.

The first is <u>structure.</u> **Structured-Talk Tools** enable conversations to be focused and safe. The second ingredient is <u>safety.</u> A **Safe-Talking Game Plan** diffuses potential volatility, and creates an environment to solve problems for good. The third ingredient is <u>boundaries.</u> A **Couple's Peace Plan** helps a couple set up boundaries to prevent conflicts from negatively impacting the health of their relationship.

The combination of these three milestones will result in authenticity, genuineness, openness, and vulnerability between a husband and wife. In essence, this is what it means to be "naked and unashamed."

Structured-Talk Tools provide couples with the necessary structure for safe conflict resolution. They help couples apply the Scripture verse in the side bar. By slowing down the conversation, couples can overcome potential miscommunication and create a safe environment for each partner to share their deep concerns or feelings. Why? As James 1:19-20 implies, how a person handles their anger dictates whether or not they experience a God-honoring life.

If that is the case, how can a couple attain the righteous life God intends for their marriage if they argue in a way that results in anger and frustration? Virtually every couple can use help to resolve conflict, raise difficult topics, and address concerns.

The first *Structured-Talk Tool* is called the **XYZ Statement.** It diffuses *Mind Reading*, *Miscommunication*, and *Negative Ways to Raise Concern*. This is how it works:

> **"When you do X..."** (specific behavior)
> **"...in situation Y..."** (specific situation)
> **"...I feel Z."** (specific feeling)

Here are examples of how the *XYZ Statement* could be used to share concerns:

 -- *"When you put me down (X) in front of your friends (Y) it makes me feel worthless (Z)."*
 -- *"When you call me at the last minute to cancel our plans, it makes me feel like the last man on the totem pole."*
 -- *"When you spend so much time on the internet, I feel neglected."*

The *XYZ Statement* can also be a means to share positive praise:

 -- *"When you compliment me in front of your friends, it makes me feel like a queen."*
 -- *"When you give me a gift when there is no holiday or anniversary to celebrate, it makes me feel loved."*

The *XYZ Statement* forces the speaker to think about the reason behind their feelings before bringing it up to their mate.

The second *Structured-Talk Tool* is called, the **Speaker-Listener Technique***. It provides structure to a conversation, helping with overall communication, counteracting negative patterns of resolving conflict, and allowing each person to speak fully and completely without interruption.

The rules to the *Speaker-Listener Technique* are as follows:

Speaker:
 -- Speak for yourself (no mind reading).
 -- Talk in small chunks (two or three sentences at the most).
 -- Stop and allow partner to paraphrase.

Listener:
 -- Paraphrase what you hear (do not "read between the lines").
 -- Don't rebut what speaker says. Focus on what they are saying.

Switch:
 -- Listener now becomes Speaker, and Speaker becomes the Listener.

In the following example of the *Speaker-Listener Technique*, the man starts as the speaker and the woman starts as the listener:

> **Man:** *"I am getting nervous about how high our credit card bill is getting."*
> **Woman:** *"You are concerned over the amount of debt we are in."*
> **Man:** *"Yes, I am thinking we need to adjust our monthly budget and get aggressive with paying the card off."*
> **Woman:** *"You want to adjust our budget so we can pay off the card faster."*
> **Man:** *"Yes."*

SWITCH

> **Woman:** *"I have been concerned about our debt for about a year."*
> **Man:** *"You share my concerns over our debt."*
> **Woman:** *"I must admit, I'm not excited about cutting the clothing budget or eating out budget because that is what I do with my girlfriends."*
> **Man:** *"You are worried about losing time with your friends by cutting our budget down."*
> **Woman:** *"Yes."*

*Used by permission of Christian PREP, Inc. Adapted from the book, *A Lasting Promise* (1998).

"The first duty of love is to listen."
-- Paul Tillich,
Protestant theologian

"Your objective as a married couple is to love and support one another as partners through good times and bad. 'Until death' can be a long time if you're obsessing over every wrongly squeezed toothpaste tube or every visit to the in-laws. You can choose to be happily married or you can choose to be miserably married."
-- Judge Judy Sheindlin,
author of Keep It Simple Stupid

Although it can feel mechanical and unnatural at first, the *Speaker-Listener Technique* allows for each person to be fully heard, fully understood, and fully aware of what the other person is feeling.

■ **What do you view as the benefits of using the XYZ Statement? What are its downfalls?**

■ **Write out a couple of (positive, praise-oriented) XYZ Statements to your mate.**

■ **What do you see as the benefits of using the Speaker-Listener Technique? What are its downfalls?**

DAY FOUR   A Game Plan for Safe Problem Solving

When a couple argues, what is typically the goal? To win! While this argument philosophy works in the courtroom between lawyers, on the university campus among debaters, or on the political campaign among political opponents, it is disastrous in a marriage. Winning arguments at all costs results in a lose-lose-lose situation for a husband, a wife, and a marriage.

In relationships, problems often arise at the wrong time, get glazed over too often, discussed infrequently, "solved" too quickly, and almost always reappear at another inopportune time. Many couples' tendency is to sidestep discussing the problem and prematurely delve into solving the problem.

Every couple needs to be able to discuss and solve problems that arise between them. By slowing down the process, and breaking the discussion into realistic steps, the chances to constructively and thoroughly solve problems greatly increase. This process is called the ***Safe-Talking Game Plan****:

> **1. Focus on the problem**
> **2. Focus on prayer**
> **3. Focus on the solution**

*Used by permission of Christian PREP, Inc. Adapted from the book, *A Lasting Promise* (1998).

The first step of the *Safe-Talking Game Plan* is to <u>focus on the problem</u>. It is important that the couple discuss specifics with the problem and avoid talking about other issues. (The *XYZ Statement* or the *Speaker-Listener Technique* creates the necessary structure to remain focused.) The goal of this part of the Game Plan is to understand, to be understood, and to create the best chances for resolution.

Once the problem has been fully discussed, spend time to <u>focus on prayer</u> together and/or individually on the matter. This allows for God to speak to the issue. If the time spent focusing on the problem has left the couple emotionally drained, take a break (later that day or another day) before trying to focus on the solution. This part of the *Game Plan* could be viewed as the intermission.

Both the husband and wife must be ready emotionally, physically, and spiritually when it is time to <u>focus on the solution</u>. This demands teamwork so to ensure the problem has truly been resolved. For this part of the *Game Plan* to be successful, there are five necessary steps on which to focus.

> **1-- Agenda:** pick a specific piece of the issue that you are working to solve.
> **2--Brainstorm:** suggest ideas without criticism or evaluation. Record all ideas on paper.
> **3-- Compromise:** work through the brainstorm ideas. Write different combinations of the ideas. Try for a specific solution that would work in light of the problem discussed.
> **4-- Deadline:** set up a time frame to try the solution, and a time to meet to evaluate the solution.
> **5-- Evaluation:** discuss the matter at an agreed upon time to determine if the solution is working or is riddled with old and/or new problems.

What are the benefits of the Safe-Talking Game Plan? What could be viewed as its weaknesses?

List 8-10 topics you think married couples argue about most.

What are some current topics you and your mate could use with this Safe-Talking Game Plan?

marriage factoid

"In studies of 700 miserable, ready-to-split spouses, researchers found that two-thirds of those who stayed married were happy five years later. They toughed out some of the most difficult problems a couple could face ... Their strategy? A mix of stubborn commitment, a willingness to work together on issues, and a healthy lowering of expectations."

-- Prevention Magazine

worthy quote

"We thought that concealing our disagreements would spare them (the children) unnecessary pain and insecurity. Now I'm not sure our approach was entirely correct. The girls have said that never seeing us argue left them wide open for surprise and disillusionment when the inevitable conflicts flared between them and their husbands. When the harmony of their households was disrupted, they assumed their marriages weren't normal."
-- Billy Graham, *evangelist*

DAY FIVE | The Couple's Peace Plan

Over the course of a lifetime together, couples can anticipate times of high stress, disagreements, and personal challenges. Knowing that it is coming, why not plan for it?

Creating a **Couple's Peace Plan*** is a proactive way to diffuse conflict before it occurs. By pre-planning how conflict will be dealt with when it occurs, couples set up boundaries for the relationship and ground rules to maintain peace in the marriage. *The Couple's Peace Plan* is a protective step to help foster respect in all situations, and protect all aspects of the relationship.

Below is an example of a *Couple's Peace Plan:*

John & Jane Doe's Peace Plan
"If it is possible, as far as it depends on you, live at peace with everyone."
Romans 12:18

We agree *that we will attempt to keep our marriage as conflict-free as possible. When conflict does occur, this is our plan to deal with it constructively, agreed upon on July 29, 2005.*

We will *regularly schedule meetings to discuss relationship-related issues.*

We declare *date nights and special times together conflict-free by agreeing not to discuss conflict-potential issues during these reserved times.*

We commit *to deal with conflict or agree upon a time to discuss conflict before going to sleep at night.*

We agree *that if a conflict issue is brought up, the other spouse can defer the discussion for an agreed upon later time set by that spouse.*

We agree *when conflict arises and is escalating, we will call a time out.*

We will *avoid participating in any Fighting Games.*

We commit *to attacking the issue, and not the person.*

We vow *never to use the word "divorce" in heated discussions.*

We will *use Structured Talk Tools (XYZ Statement or Speaker-Listener Technique) when we are having trouble communicating.*

We agree *to use the Safe Talking Game Plan to separate problem discussion from problem solving.*

We commit *to praying before, during and after dealing with conflict.*

The *Couple's Peace Plan* is intended to give couples principles to live by at the time they are needed most. These agreed-upon rules must be established when conflict is absent and tensions are minimal.

By applying structure to potentially-heated discussions, conflict can be beneficial to the relationship. An ounce of prevention (in one's speech, actions, and attitudes) will result in tons of harmony, unity, and joy in the marriage.

*Used by permission of Christian PREP, Inc. Adapted from the book, *A Lasting Promise* (1998).

What does your current "peace plan" look like
(agreed upon rules)?

What rules should be added to expand your current peace plan?

List up to ten statements you would like to have in your
Couple's Peace Plan.

Is there a Scripture verse, a popularized saying, or a created phrase
that could act as a master statement for your Couple's Peace Plan?

DAY SIX | Couple Time - Discussion Questions

Take some time to discuss *Fight With Your Mate & Please God Too* with one another. In addition to the questions below are some suggestions for practicing the skills you just learned. Write down points of agreement, disagreement or issues to further discuss.

- *On a scale of 1 to 10 (1=poor, 10=great), how good are you and your mate at resolving conflict?*

- *How often does conflict arise with your mate? Do issues get resolved or stay unresolved? Why?*

- *Discuss which Fighting Games are most popular in your relationship. What triggers them?*

- *Which Fighting Games were most present in your family during your growing-up years?*

- *What contributes most often to Mixed Messages in your relationship?*

- *Practice the XYZ Statement with one another with a neutral topic.*

- *Practice the Speaker-Listener Technique with a topic pertaining to your wedding. Keep the rules open in front of you.*

- *Apply the following scenario and practice the Safe-Talking Game Plan (discuss problem using the Speaker-Listener Technique and solve problems using the five steps to focus on the solution).*

    The woman in this scenario is emphatic that the toilet paper rolls over the top. The man doesn't care which way it rolls, causing irritation in the relationship. Roll play taking 90 seconds each to discuss the problem and then work on solving it.

- *Write your own Couple's Peace Plan.*

Marriage Investor Session Notes

DAY SEVEN

Use this space to capture notes, thoughts, and issues that arise while meeting with your Marriage Investor.

Go Deeper

At **www.FullMarriageExperience.com** you will find lists of helpful books and articles, informative web sites, and practical resources related to topics covered in this section.

■ *Conflict Resolution*
■ *Communication*

Section 5

Ensure the "I Do's" Last a Lifetime

"Hollywood's Happy Couples!"

The grocery checkout-stand rag dubbed several of Tinseltown's most popular husband and wife duos with the title above. Within a few years, the featured couples had all separated, divorced, and begun new relationships.

In a day and age when one-in-three couples opt to dissolve their marriage rather than resolve their relationship issues, many ask, *"why is divorce so prominent when we place so much focus on love?"*

Choices. After making one monumental decision ("I do"), the rest of a couple's life is filled with making meaningful, smaller choices. Communities used to support and encourage couples to make choices that put others' interests first.

In the late-sixties, divorce laws changed making it easier for one spouse to decide to end what took two people to begin. Divorces skyrocketed in the seventies and eighties, and plateaued in the nineties. Millions of kids have been impacted. Current conditions explain why this era has been called "the divorce culture."

Everyone has felt the impact of divorce, whether it has involved a family member, a friend, co-worker, or a celebrity. The divorce culture has created an unhealthy environment for marriages and an eroding marriage landscape. As onlookers witness couples moving down the marriage-to-divorce conveyor belt, many think, *"if it happened to them, it could happen to me."*

So how does a couple enter into a marriage and avoid taking the path-way that one-third of all married couples end up trekking down? Choices.

This section, ***Ensure the "I Do's" Last a Lifetime***, informs couples how to overcome common obstacles that trip-up too many marriages. This section helps couples identify choices that cause barriers to a vibrant marriage and recognize healthy choices to build a relationship that goes the distance. Learning to communicate, deepen intimacy, protect friendship, and forgive will all but ensure a couple lives the *Full Marriage Experience*.

███ ***How does living in a divorce culture affect your view of marriage?***

DAY ONE

Six Choices that Breed Marriage Barriers

the Bible says

"When the Woman saw that the tree looked like good eating and realized what she would get out of it - she'd know everything! - she took and ate the fruit and then gave some to her husband, and he ate. Immediately the two of them did 'see what's really going on' - saw themselves naked! They sewed fig leaves together as makeshift clothes for themselves. When they heard the sound of God strolling in the garden in the evening breeze, the Man and his Wife hid in the trees of the garden, hid from God. God called to the Man: 'Where are you?' He said, 'I heard you in the garden and I was afraid because I was naked. And I hid.' God said, 'Who told you you were naked? Did you eat from that tree I told you not to eat from?' The Man said, 'The Woman you gave me as a companion, she gave me fruit from the tree, and, yes, I ate it.' God said to the Woman, 'What is this that you've done?' 'The serpent seduced me,' she said, 'and I ate.'"
Genesis 3:6-13

a closer look

To Overcome the Choice to Remain Uninformed:
-- *Read books about relationship issues*
-- *Attend marriage conferences*
-- *Spend time with older couples*
-- *Learn relationship skills that benefit the marriage*

a closer look

To Overthrow the Choice of Disregard:
-- *Prioritize life—God first, spouse second, and self third*
-- *Read the Scriptures regularly*
-- *Pray often*
-- *Identify sin in one's own life*
-- *Seek forgiveness*
-- *Embrace God's restoration*
-- *Find friends who can trustfully help with accountability*

The previous sections have highlighted God's instructions, principles, and insight to live the *Full Marriage Experience*. God's ideal for marriage is available to any couple, if they so choose.

Soon after God established His plan for marriage, things changed drastically. According to Genesis 3:6-13, tragedy hit the Garden of Eden. The relationship between husband and wife would be forever changed. The fallout from eating the forbidden fruit created instant barriers in the relationship between husband and wife and the relationship between the couple and their Creator. These relationship barriers resulted from choices made by both Adam and Eve.

These same barriers can impact any marriage, at any time, during any season of life. The barriers result from six choices that individuals and couples make. By identifying the choices, couples can recognize them, overcome them or avoid them entirely. The *Six Choices that Breed Marriage Barriers** are **the Choice to Remain Uninformed, the Choice of Disregard, the Choice to Cover-Up, the Choice of Extreme Insecurity, the Choice of Hyper-Selfishness, and the Blame & Shame Choice.**

THE CHOICE TO REMAIN UNINFORMED: Ignorance occurs when couples charter on the unfamiliar waters of life together without help or guidance from others. By being uninformed or unknowledgeable of God's principles for their relationship, couples will lack the skills necessary to expand the scope of their role in growing the marriage relationship. Remaining uninformed that a relationship can improve may cause mates to feel desperate and anxious and, over time, smother out the intimacy and joy they feel.

 *How has the Choice to Remain Uninformed acted as a barrier in your relationship with your mate?*

THE CHOICE OF DISREGARD: This choice means to blatantly disregard others or God by doing something a person knows they should not do or refuse to do something they know they should do. Fueling this choice is the desire to satisfy one's own desires regardless of the impact on other people. Often referred to as "sin," it is the root of all relational problems with God and others.

Eve had been instructed by the Creator not to eat the fruit from a certain tree. The fruit appealed to her eyes. She decided to disregard God, because she believed the fruit would make her god-like. Her desire to satisfy her own wants usurped her desire to obey God's instruction.

In marriage, if a couple ignores guidance, disregards direction, or rebuffs help, the health of the relationship suffers immensely.

How has the Choice of Disregard bred barriers in your relationship?

*Used by permission of Christian PREP, Inc. Adapted from the book, *A Lasting Promise* (1998).

THE CHOICE TO COVER-UP: Nobody likes being exposed. Almost instinctively, people protect themselves by accentuating their strengths, talents, skills, and successes while covering up their areas of weakness, faults, misgivings, and pasts.

When Adam and Eve clothed themselves with fig leaves, the couple didn't hide the eyes that saw the fruit, the hands that grabbed the fruit, nor the mouth that ate the fruit. Each hid the anatomical parts that were distinctly different from the other. When a sense of self-preservation exists between a husband and wife, the *Choice to Cover-Up* is a challenge on too many marriages.

■ *How has the Choice to Cover-Up acted as a barrier in your relationship with your mate?*

To Overcome the Choice to Cover Up:
-- *Spend quality time together*
-- *Speak to one another with constructive talk*
-- *Use structured talk tools at times of conflict*
-- *Accept each others' faults, misgivings, and pasts*

THE CHOICE OF EXTREME INSECURITY: Every person lives with a certain amount of insecurity fueled by a fear of being rejected by others.

When the full realization of eating the fruit came upon them, Adam and Eve looked out for their own interests first. It occurred when they sought out the fig leaves. Then they hid when God came looking for them. Everyone has a tendency to protect themselves from others. Whether out of a fear of rejection or protecting one's pride, extreme insecurity is a major barrier from deepening intimacy in the marriage relationship.

■ *How has the Choice of Extreme Insecurity acted as a barrier in your relationship with your mate?*

To Overtake the Choice of Extreme Insecurity:
-- *Build new levels of trust in the relationship*
-- *Deny one's insecurity for the sake of the relationship*
-- *Accept one another for who they really are*
-- *Share freely about one's dreams, hopes, and fears*
-- *Refrain from exposing each other's secrets to others*

THE CHOICE OF HYPER-SELFISHNESS: The basis of every bad thing in the Garden Story begins with selfishness: the act of eating the fruit, the attempts to hide from one another, and the excuses Adam and Eve gave to God. In marriage there is no quicker way to unravel the fabric of love, trust, and commitment than to be selfish in a relationship intended to be selfless at its core.

■ *How has the Choice of Hyper-Selfishness acted as a barrier in your relationship with your mate?*

To Overthrow the Choice of Hyper-Selfishness:
-- *Seek to honor one's spouse above oneself*
-- *Ask daily, "what can I do for my mate today?"*
-- *Evaluate how actions and speech are affecting one's partner*
-- *Determine one's impact and influence on spouse*

a closer look

To Overcome the Blame & Shame Choice:
-- *Accept responsibility for one's own actions and words*
-- *Choose not to blame others, especially one's spouse*
-- *Refrain from shaming anyone*

THE BLAME & SHAME CHOICE: When bad things occur, the first thing people do is look for someone or something to blame (e.g. *"The co-worker flaked." "The computer crashed."*) Blame is intrinsic in everyone.

When God confronted Adam, not only did the man shift the accusation to Eve, but he also indicted God for making the woman (in case God didn't buy the "Eve-scapegoat excuse"). Noticing that the options to shift blame were waning, Eve pointed her finger at the serpent.

Blaming one's mate and hoisting shame on them for all the relationship's faults, or one's own personal weaknesses is a sure-fire way to undermine the quality of the marriage relationship.

 How has the Blame & Shame Choice bred a barrier in your relationship with your mate?

take a note

Six Choices that Breed Marriage Barriers:

-- *Choice to Remain Uninformed*
-- *Choice of Disregard*
-- *Choice to Cover-Up*
-- *Choice of Extreme Insecurity*
-- *Choice of Hyper-Selfishness*
-- *Blame & Shame Choice*

The *Six Choices that Breed Marriage Barriers* are not exclusively reserved for after the wedding date. Either partner can make these choices during difficult times, moments of temporary tragedy or during relatively calm seasons of the relationship. They can even be made during the high peaks and seasons of life. The result is always the same, an invisible but evident wall separates the couple keeping them from living the *Full Marriage Experience*.

Which Six Choices that Breed Marriage Barriers concern you?

How might these choices impact the quality of your marriage?

DAY TWO   Four Choices that Guarantee a Lifetime

While the *Six Choices that Breed Marriage Barriers* should be avoided, there are four other choices that must be made. These choices have a positive effect on the relationship, and give couples the best chance for their "I do's" to last a lifetime.

The Four Choices that Guarantee a Lifetime are: the **Choice to Communicate, the Choice to Deepen Intimacy, the Choice to Protect Friendship, and the Choice to Forgive.**

The Choice to Communicate

While many relationships between men and women are conceived in physical attraction and romance, the relationship must grow with heart and skill. The primary method of sharing one's heart is with the mouth and ears. Therefore it is essential that couples know how to communicate with one another effectively.

Just because each person in the relationship has a set of lips, a pair of ears, and a brain does not mean communication is taking place. Marriage is a combination of facts, feelings, experiences, thoughts, hopes, dreams, and day-to-day life. Choosing to debrief, discuss, share, and talk are not only advantages of being involved in a lifelong relationship, they are necessities.

Communication goes beyond the mere words a person says. Body language, tone of voice, specific words used and not used are all part of conveying and receiving messages. Common knowledge says that 60 percent of communication is body language, 25 percent is the tone of voice, and the remaining 15 percent is the actual words themselves. This amplifies the importance of knowing how to talk to one another.

The context of a message is vital to knowing the true meaning of that message. Unlike any other relationship, how a mate treats the other (attitudes and behaviors) substantially adds to or detracts from the words that are being spoken. The unique thing about marriage is that the two people are constantly together (minus time at work, sleeping, etc.).

For example, if the husband says, *"you are the most important thing in my life,"* the wife will instantly think of the context couching that statement. If he has been working overtime at work, coming home late, spending time on the computer until bedtime, and spending the weekends fishing with friends, that phrase may not be received real well.

take a note

Communication is the entire package of how people talk to one another — the words themselves, the tone of voice in which the words are expressed, and the body language of the one speaking.

take a note

The **context** of the message — how the person speaking treats the other — will substantially add or detract from the words spoken.

■ *Which part of communication do you tend to react to most (the words, the tone, or the body language)?*

■ *Which part of communication does your mate tend to react to most (the words, the tone, or the body language)?*

■ *On a scale of 1-10 (1=lowest, 10=highest), how well do you and your mate communicate? What reasons back up your rating?*

worthy quote

"Women don't want to hear what you think. Women want to hear what they think — in a deeper voice."
-- Bill Cosby, comedian and actor

DAY THREE

The Choice to Deepen Intimacy

All relationships have a starting point, an ultimate destination (depth one desires a relationship to grow to), and a point of reality (where a relationship currently exists).

How important the relationship is, how deep the conversation goes, and how open to sharing details of one's personal life are all contributors to the level of intimacy in a particular relationship.

Intimacy in this context is not sexual or physical. Rather, it signifies the emotional connection and levels of communication. It is based on the rate of honest self-disclosure and acceptance in the relationship.

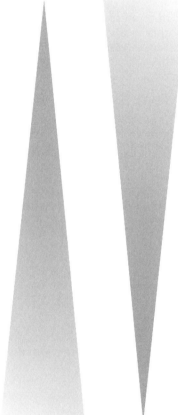

Number of People

Degree of Intimacy

HIGHEST LEVEL: Everything
This level is sharing deep feelings and emotions; being transparent at all levels.
  "This is who I really am."

HIGH LEVEL: My Background
This level is divulging personal values, dreams, and goals that are important and sacred.
  "As long as I can remember, I have always wanted to fly."

MODERATE LEVEL: My Ideas
This level is offering your ideas and opinions that are changeable; offering a portion of one's self.
  "I believe the media are biased."

LOW LEVEL: Ideas of Others
This level of talk offers the ideas and opinions of others for personal safety from judgment.
  "Ed thinks actors earn too much."

LOWEST LEVEL: Surface
This lowest level of talk is sharing basic facts that offer no personal details or investment.
  "It's a nice day today."

There is a limit to how many people a single person can deepen intimacy with. Notice that the deeper the level of intimacy, the fewer numer of people one can share it with.

This is due to the fact that as intimacy with a person intensifies, it takes more time to maintain it at that level. In order to spend the necessary time with an individual (or a few people) one must take time away from investing into other potential relationships.

The highest level of intimacy should be the goal for all marriage relationships. All other levels of intimacy in other relationships should pale in comparison.

The **Choice to Deepen Intimacy** to the highest levels with one's spouse will prioritize every other relationship in its appropriate standing. This will alleviate undue pressure and imbalance in the relationship.

> *What level of intimacy do you now experience with your mate? How can you grow it (even if you rate it at the highest level)?*

> *Place the name(s) of people (other than your mate) you have a relationship with at the different levels of intimacy.*
>
> *-- Highest:*
>
> *-- High:*
>
> *-- Moderate:*
>
> *-- Low:*
>
> *-- Lowest:*

> *How will intimacy levels with other people change after marriage?*

The desire for growing deeper intimacy with one's spouse exists in the heart-of-hearts of most everyone. It doesn't happen by accident. It takes initiative, willingness, and desire.

Making the *Choice to Deepen Intimacy* will result in meaningful conversations, deeper feelings of connectedness, and higher levels of empathy. These are all vital ingredients for couples to live the *Full Marriage Experience*.

worthy quote

"So you learn to accept each other. Your best behavior is now and forever reserved for outside the house, and once you're inside, you're free to be the repellent American you really are ...You become a little team. It's the 'two of you' against 'everybody else.' And you look out for each other. Your partner becomes the one person in the world you can go over to and say, 'Do I have anything in my nose?' ... That's their little privilege."
-- Paul Reiser, comedian and actor

marriage factoid

" When it comes to avoiding misery, a wedding band helps. Married men and women report less depression, less anxiety, and lower levels of other types of psychological distress than do those who are single, divorced, or widowed."

-- The Case for Marriage

worthy quote

"In healthy marriages, men and women seek to perfect themselves for the sake of the other. Day in and day out, they offer and draw moral strength, sharing compassion, courage, honesty, self-discipline, and a host of other virtues. The whole of the union becomes stronger than the sum of the parts."
-- William J. Bennett, former Secretary of Education

DAY FOUR

The Choice to Protect Friendship

In the beginning stages of a relationship, couples spend their time together experiencing new and exciting activities. Time together is time away from work, from school, and from other responsibilities. That is what makes the early stages of a relationship fun.

When a couple gets engaged, things change a bit. The fun times compete with wedding planning time (which, depending on circumstances, can either be fun or a drudgery). Planning the event, registering for gifts, meeting with vendors, and handling all the details surrounding the wedding become, for many couples, the first time when real life details mesh with and infringe on the frolicking fun of the dating days. This is not a bad thing; in fact, it is a healthy transition for the relationship.

After the wedding day is over, the thank-you cards have been mailed, and wedding gifts have been opened - the difficult task of balancing work-life, other friendships, family obligations, hobbies, and the marriage relationship begins. The wedding distractions have been replaced with the distractions of the real world. Yes, real life has entered the home and the relationship of this loving couple.

Over time, friendship in marriage can slip away due to job transitions, buying a home, paying bills, and the rest of the daily grind. No couple lets it slip away intentionally. But if the stresses of life dominate the relationship, and a perception of conflict looms in the air, the times for conversation tend to be avoided. Friendship is one of the first things to be affected when a relationship gives way to stress.

Making the **Choice to Protect Friendship*** is vital to the health of the marriage. People don't get married to become consumed with life's pressures and lose focus on their relationship. Yet, too many couples neglect the friendship part of their relationship. They can become married singles (still married but have separate lives), emotionally divorced, or stuck in a relationship void of any real joy.

What can a couple do to protect friendship? Choose. Here's how.

- **Make time for fun!** Set regular date nights on the calendar, try new things together, and reserve times during the week for uninterrupted, meaningful time together.

- **Protect your time!** Couples need to protect their "fun time" from two things: other people and conflict. People can be a drain on your relationship by wanting alone time with one of you, or continually spending time with both of you. Learn to keep healthy balance and boundaries with other people.

  Also, protect date nights or fun times by avoiding discussion on issues that lead to fights. It is a guaranteed way to undo any positives created by spending time together.

- **Be a friend and act like it!** A spouse is not only a partner and lover, they are also a friend. Treat them better than all other friends. Treating one's spouse with less importance than another friend is to reveal where they fall in the pecking order of priorities and worth.

*Used by permission of Christian PREP, Inc. Adapted from the book, *A Lasting Promise* (1998).

Intimacy grows by deepening the friendship between husband and wife. Friendship is fostered by sharing fun and enjoyable experiences. Make the *Choice to Protect Friendship* and you are one choice closer to living the *Full Marriage Experience*.

What do you and your mate currently do for fun? What fun things do you want to try as a couple after you are married?

What challenges do you foresee that could jeopardize your fun time?

How will you protect your fun time after you are married?

How will you grow a deeper friendship with your mate after you are married?

List friends you will spend time together with as a couple. List friends you will spend time with separately.

Do you view any of your friends or your mate's friends as risks to the health of your marriage relationship?

"Friendship is a single soul dwelling in two bodies."
-- Aristotle, *Greek philosopher*

"You will enjoy your marriage more if you laugh a lot together. Try to find ways to experience pleasure that endears you to each other ... Develop secrets together, private jokes that keep you whispering fun nothings and keep you intrigued with each other. Wink at him and watch him melt. He'll love it. Schedule time to go out and do something fun, even if your budget is tight. Be creative. Find ways to make fun happen. Instead of thinking, Oh we can't do that! Find a way; be persistent and watch your dreams come true."
-- Linda Weber, *author of Mom, You're Incredible*

DAY FIVE

the Bible says

"Summing up: Be agreeable, be sympathetic, be loving, be compassionate, be humble. That goes for all of you, no exceptions. No retaliation. No sharp-tongued sarcasm. Instead, bless —that's your job, to bless. You'll be a blessing and also get a blessing.

Whoever wants to embrace life and see the day fill up with good, here's what you do: Say nothing evil or hurtful; Snub evil and cultivate good; run after peace for all you're worth. God looks on all this with approval, listening and responding well to what he's asked; But he turns his back on those who do evil things."
I Peter 3:9-11

take a note

Forgiveness means to cancel the debt of another person.

the Bible says

"Be even-tempered, content with second place, quick to forgive an offense. Forgive as quickly and completely as the Master forgave you."
Colossians 3:13

take a note

Reconciliation means to make things right with another person, to bring the relationship to the same place it was before the infraction.

The Choice to Forgive

Even though a couple can be highly knowledgeable of communication skills, ways to grow intimacy, and how to protect friendship in their marriage, they are human. Stuff happens. Mistakes are made. Miscommunication occurs. Even with the best of intentions, a husband and wife will fail one another at some point.

What happens when this occurs? Some hold grudges. Some keep a growing record of all past hurts and bring it up at convenient times. Others let it fall off of them and never address the issue. All of these are destructive to the long-term well-being of a marriage relationship.

Any marriage that lasts a lifetime must have a pattern of forgiveness sewn into its seams. The **Choice to Forgive** means to cancel the debt of another person. Don't confuse forgiveness with forgetting. When one grants forgiveness to another person, they are laying down the desire for revenge. Memory of past hurts are a part of life. But indefinitely holding them against another is no way to heal, no way to restore a relationship, and no way to live the *Full Marriage Experience*.

Forgiveness does not mean that the person committing an offense is not responsible for the consequences of their behavior. People must be responsible for their actions, and they must be held accountable. This allows the entire process of reconciliation and restoration to take place which builds trust in the relationship.

Here are some helpful steps to activate forgiveness*.

-- Pray to God for wisdom and a pure heart.

-- Determine a safe time to discuss the issue.

-- Allow the offended party to share concerns and feelings.

-- Admit fault, apologize, and ask for forgiveness if you are the offender. (Saying "I'm sorry" is not enough as it places the responsibility on the offended rather than the offender.)

-- Agree to forgive the offender.

-- Make a commitment to change and develop a plan to address any recurrent patterns.

-- Pray and move forward.

To reconcile means to make things right with another person, to bring the relationship to the same place it was before the infraction. For the well being of the marriage relationship, couples must not simply gloss over issues. By raising the standard for forgiveness, reconciliation becomes a part of the marriage. It will take more time. It will demand more effort. It will require more energy. But the *Choice to Forgive* will pay off great dividends over the course of a lifetime.

*Used by permission of Christian PREP, Inc. Adapted from the book, *A Lasting Promise* (1998).

Are you holding grudges against anyone (not including your mate) right now? If so, who and why?

What is standing in the way of extending forgiveness to them?

Do you know of anyone (other than your mate) who is holding grudges against you? If so, who and why?

Are there any grudges or resentment, issues or experiences for which you need to forgive your partner? List them below.

Are there any grudges or resentment, issues or experiences for which you partner needs to forgive you? List them below.

" *Forgiving love safeguards your marriage by healing hurts and helping you feel accepted and connected ... it's a love that is securely rooted in God's love for us ... When you exhibit the grace of forgiving love toward your spouse, you change the entire tone of your marriage. No longer are you like referees counting each other's fouls, ready to toss each other out of the game. Marriage becomes a safe place where you don't have to hide your foibles and your failings. Instead of feeling scrutinized and condemned for your shortcomings, you feel accepted and forgiven.*"
-- Gary & Barbara Rosberg, *America's Family Coaches*

Choices. Couples will have ample opportunities to say "I do" to the *Four Choices that Guarantee a Lifetime*: the *Choice to Communicate*, the *Choice to Deepen Intimacy*, the *Choice to Protect Friendship*, and the *Choice to Forgive*. They also will have an abundance of opportunities to choose one of the *Six Choices that Breed Marriage Barriers*.

The decisions will need to be made numerous times on a daily basis. Which set of Choices are ultimately chosen will determine the couple's probability of living the *Full Marriage Experience*.

"All those 'and they lived happily ever after' fairy tale endings need to be changed to 'and they began the very hard work of making their marriage happy.'"
-- Linda Miles, *author of 8 Keys to Lasting Love*

DAY SIX Couple Time - Discussion Questions

Take some time to discuss **Ensure the "I Do's" Last a Lifetime** with one another. Use the following questions and suggestions as a guide.

- *Discuss which of the Six Choices that Breed Marriage Barriers you saw most often in your parents' relationship*

- *What contributes most often to barriers in your relationship?*

- *What steps will you take to break down any existing barriers in your relationship?*

- *How will you avoid the Six Choices that Breed Marriage Barriers in the future?*

- *How can you improve communication in your relationship?*

- *Think about the people who have been at the highest levels of intimacy over your lifetime. What do they have in common? Why did you invest so much of yourself in them?*

- *Discuss how you will determine if friendship is suffering in your relationship? What will trigger you to make changes?*

- *Discuss how you and your mate will activate forgiveness in your marriage.*

Marriage Investor Session Notes

DAY SEVEN

Use this space to capture notes, thoughts, and issues that arise while meeting with your Marriage Investor.

Go Deeper

At **www.FullMarriageExperience.com** you will find lists of helpful books and articles, informative web sites, and practical resources related to topics covered in this section.

■ *Communication*
■ *Forgiveness*
■ *Intimacy*
■ *Friendship*
■ *Fun*

Section 6

Walk on the Spiritual Side of Marriage

A church-sponsored billboard advertisement displays a note card with a handwritten message, "Loved the wedding! How about inviting me into the marriage? - God."

The above public service announcement conveys to couples the importance faith has in their marriage.

Weddings and churches, marriage and religion, families and houses of worship: historically, these associations have gone hand-in-hand. Recently, these associations have been less apparent. Does it really matter? Do religious faith, spiritual beliefs, the Bible, God, or the church make much of a difference in marriage?

Many couples have experienced the positive impact of religious faith in their marriage. Some claim it helped them avoid trauma, while others say faith is what got them through hard times. Recent studies confirm that an active religious faith contributes to the health, longevity, and well-being of a marriage relationship.

Yet divorce happens in the religious community. Adultery occurs among people of faith. Unhealthy and unsafe relationships exist in some religious homes. Couples have even broken up over religion. So why the apparent contradiction?

Just because someone possesses a religious faith does not mean they are perfect, nor does it guarantee a married life of heavenly bliss. Unhealthy relationships exist both inside and outside the church.

Choices determine whether faith has a positive or negative effect on the relationship. The ultimate choice of faith's role in the relationship must be made individually by the man and the woman, and then as a couple. Their decision dictates faith's effect on their marriage.

This section, **Walk on the Spiritual Side of Marriage**, helps couples discuss issues related to faith and their relationship. Couples will look at the *Faith-Effect on Marriage*, dig into their separate spiritual histories, and determine how God's Divine Hand has touched the relationship. Couples will also explore several ways to grow spiritually together so they live the *Full Marriage Experience*.

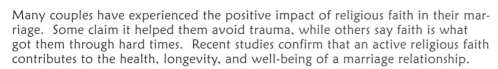

■ *In general, do you have a positive, neutral, or negative view toward religious faith? Why?*

DAY ONE

The Faith-Effect on Marriage

the Bible says

"So here's what I want you to do, God helping you: Take your everyday, ordinary life — your sleeping, eating, going-to-work, and walking-around life — and place it before God as an offering. Embracing what God does for you is the best thing you can do for Him. Don't become so well-adjusted to your culture that you fit into it without even thinking. Instead, fix your attention on God. You'll be changed from the inside out. Readily recognize what He wants from you, and quickly respond to it. Unlike the culture around you, always dragging you down to its level of immaturity, God brings the best out of you, develops well-formed maturity in you."
Romans 12:1-2

worthy quote

"I can never again believe that religion is manufactured out of our unconscious, starved desires … For those few years H. (his wife Helen Joy) and I feasted on love … solemn and merry, romantic and realistic … No cranny of heart or body remained unsatisfied. If God were a substitute for love, we ought to have lost all interest in Him … But that isn't what happens. We both … wanted something besides one another … a different kind of something … different kind of want … The most precious gift that marriage gave me was this constant impact of something very close and intimate yet all the time … real."
-- C.S. Lewis, author of The Chronicles of Narnia

The faith community has developed a large number of resources and services to help couples grow in their marriage relationship. Books have been written, seminars have been created, enrichment retreats have been started, and service organizations have been formed.

Over the last several decades, studies have measured the impact of religious beliefs, religious practices (e.g., prayer and Bible reading), religious activity, and spirituality on the overall health and longevity of the marriage relationship.

What researchers have discovered can be called the *Faith-Effect on Marriage*. "Encounter God Together" is one of the ten ideals for couples to live the *Full Marriage Experience*. Faith makes a positive contribution to many areas of the marriage relationship, including attitudes, behaviors, and overall well-being.

A spouse's attitude fuels their actions in the relationship. A spouse's behavior influences the perceived and realized well-being of the relationship.

-- **ATTITUDES:** Practicing religion is a great contributor to marital happiness. Faith impacts a spouse's personal commitment to their marriage relationship, and their belief in the institution of marriage.

Religiously practicing couples tend to have less favorable views towards divorce as an option in their relationship.

-- **BEHAVIORS:** Couples "satisfied with how they express their spiritual values and beliefs" are more likely to rate resolving conflict, communication and financial management as strengths in their marriage relationship.

Unfortunately, conflict in marriage sometimes leads couples to file for divorce. The rate of divorce is more than two times higher for couples who do not regularly attend religious services than for couples who attend services weekly.

In some relationships, conflict can also result in domestic violence. In relationships with men who attend religious services regularly, the occurrence of violence against women is half as likely than when men attend once a year or less. Religious activity ensures greater likelihood of being in a violence-free relationship.

Couples who share a common faith report a higher level of sexual satisfaction. According to one of the most extensive surveys on sex, the most sexually satisfied person in America is a married woman with a deep, personal faith.

-- **WELL-BEING:** Couples who share a common faith have a greater propensity to be married for a lifetime. Attending religious services is one of the most important factors to a couple's happiness.

Couples with long lasting marriages express that their religious faith has been an important factor in their marital satisfaction and stability.

Marital adjustment and longevity are significantly affected by religion and spirituality. In fact, married couples with the lowest risk of divorce are those who attend church together regularly.

■ **What are your initial reactions to the Faith-Effect on Marriage?**

■ **Why do you think the research reflects such a difference between religious and non-religious couples in the various marriage areas?**

■ **How does the Faith-Effect on Marriage affect your view of religious faith in your relationship?**

"In their massive study of American sexual behavior titled, The Social Organization of Sexuality (1994), Laumann, Gagnon, Michael, and Michaels reported that those couples who frequently attend religious services are only one half as likely to divorce as those who do not attend."

take a note

The Faith-Effect on Marriage impacts several areas of a couple's relationship.

-- Attitudes
-- Behavior
-- Well-being

Charting Your Spiritual Journey   DAY TWO

Whether you realize it or not, everyone possesses spiritual beliefs. The atheist and the fundamentalist may be on opposite sides of the religious spectrum, but both have deep-seated spiritual beliefs.

These beliefs affect actions, thoughts, and speech. Spiritual beliefs can go even deeper by providing people with stability in an ever-changing world, hope in a hopeless generation, and encouragement in the face of a negatively-charged life.

Spiritual beliefs are deeply personal. The deeper the intimacy within the marriage relationship, the greater impact those spiritual beliefs will have on the quality of the relationship.

On the next page is a chart of spiritual beliefs. Respond to the questions by writing answers in the box. To the best of your ability, answer the questions for yourself (in the first column) and your mate (in the second column). In the third column, determine if you and your mate share the same belief, a similar belief, or a different belief.

People who considered themselves atheists participated in the following religious activities in the last seven days.

-- Attended church services = 4%
-- Read Bible = 9%
-- Prayed to God = 27%

-- **www.barna.org**

Charting Your Spiritual Beliefs

	You	Mate	
GOD BELIEF *Atheism (no God), agnostic (don't know if God exists), monotheistic (only one God), polytheistic (many gods), pantheistic (all things are god), other?*			☐ Same ☐ Similar ☐ Different
RELIGIOUS GROUP *Christianity, Buddhism, Humanism, Judaism, Baha'i, Hinduism, New Age, Mormonism, Islam, other?*			☐ Same ☐ Similar ☐ Different
SPECIAL AFFILIATION *Do you belong to a certain denomination, grouping or sect within your religious tradition? Which one?*			☐ Same ☐ Similar ☐ Different
RELIGIOUS ACTIVITY *How often do you participate in organized religious services (daily, weekly, monthly, yearly, never)?*			☐ Same ☐ Similar ☐ Different
GOD VIEW *Do you see God as active in people's lives, watching from a distance, unconcerned about humanity, non-existent, other?*			☐ Same ☐ Similar ☐ Different
SPIRITUAL TEACHERS *Who are people (famous or not) who influence your spiritual beliefs and life?*			☐ Same ☐ Similar ☐ Different
FAITH IMPORTANCE *Rate on a scale of 1-10 (1=low, 10=high) how important your faith belief is to you.*			☐ Same ☐ Similar ☐ Different
ORIGIN OF LIFE *Do you believe in creation, evolution, or theistic evolution (God started the evolutionary process)?*			☐ Same ☐ Similar ☐ Different
LIFE & DEATH *Is there an afterlife and if so, what is it?*			☐ Same ☐ Similar ☐ Different

How many of your spiritual beliefs are the same as, similar to, and/or different from the spiritual beliefs of your mate?

How can your shared spiritual beliefs be a strength for your relationship?

How can your shared spiritual beliefs negatively affect your relationship?

How can your different spiritual beliefs be a strength for your relationship?

How can your different spiritual beliefs have a negative effect on your relationship?

How have your spiritual beliefs changed since the relationship with your mate began?

Does the relationship benefit, suffer, or experience no impact from your spiritual beliefs and those of your mate? Explain why.

Americans' religious preferences:

-- Protestant = 56%
-- Catholic = 22%
-- Atheist or
   Agnostic = 7%
-- Mormon = 2%

-- www.barna.org

the Bible says

"Dear friends, do you think you'll get anywhere in this if you learn all the right words but never do anything? Does merely talking about faith indicate that a person really has it? For instance, you come upon an old friend dressed in rags and half-starved and say, 'Good morning, friend! Be clothed in Christ! Be filled with the Holy Spirit!' and walk off without providing so much as a coat or a cup of soup —where does that get you? Isn't it obvious that God-talk without God-acts is outrageous nonsense?

I can already hear one of you agreeing by saying, 'Sounds good. You take care of the faith department, I'll handle the works department.'

Not so fast. You can no more show me your works apart from your faith than I can show you my faith apart from my works. Faith and works, works and faith, fit together hand in glove.

Do I hear you professing to believe in the one and only God, but then observe you complacently sitting back as if you had done something wonderful? That's just great. Demons do that, but what good does it do them? Use your heads! Do you suppose for a minute that you can cut faith and works in two and not end up with a corpse on your hands?

...Is it not evident that a person is made right with God not by a barren faith but by faith fruitful in works?"
James 2:14-20, 24

Your Spiritual Journey to Date

Religious views, spiritual beliefs, and convictions of faith are formed over one's entire lifetime. They result from such factors as one's upbringing, peer influences, and family traditions. Record your spiritual journey by responding to the questions and statements below.

Briefly describe your view of God and His role in your life.

What was your religious upbringing?

Did your religious upbringing (or lack of religious upbringing) have a positive, neutral, or negative impact on you? Why?

How important are spiritual matters in your life? How long have they been at this level of importance?

List people and/or experiences that have had a positive impact on your spiritual journey.

List people and/or experiences that have had a negative impact on your spiritual journey.

How do you express your spirituality on a regular basis?

marriage factoid

Americans' religious activities in the last seven days:

-- Attended church services = 43%
-- Read Bible = 38%
-- Prayed to God = 82%
-- Attended Sunday School = 16%
-- Volunteered at church = 16%
-- Donated money to church = 18%
-- Shared faith with others = 24%

-- www.barna.org

worthy quote

"Worship is response to the overtures of love from the heart of the Father. Its central reality is found 'in spirit and truth.' It is kindled within us only when the Spirit of God touches our human spirit. Forms and rituals do not produce worship, nor does the disuse of forms and rituals. We can use all the right techniques and methods, we can have the best possible liturgy, but we have not worshipped the Lord until Spirit touches spirit."
-- **Richard Foster**, writer and speaker on Christian spirituality

Your Mate's Spiritual Journey to Date

When a couple exchanges their "*I do's*," their physical, financial, and spiritual lives merge together. The following questions and statements will help you chart your mate's spiritual journey, helping you both yield enough so your spiritual paths merge, and avoid a head-on collision.

Briefly describe your mate's view of God and His role in their life.

What was your mate's religious upbringing?

Did your mate's religious upbringing (or lack of religious upbringing) have a positive, neutral, or negative impact on them? Why?

How important are spiritual matters in their life? How long have they been at this level of importance?

List people and/or experiences that have had a positive impact on your mate's spiritual journey.

List people and/or experiences that have had a negative impact on your mate's spiritual journey.

How does your mate express their spirituality on a regular basis?

Americans' attendance at religious services:

-- Once a week or more = 40%
-- Seldom or never = 24%
-- A few times a year = 18%
-- Once or twice a month = 17%

-- REV! Magazine

DAY THREE

Merging Spiritual Paths

It is not uncommon for partners to come from different religious backgrounds and upbringings. The marriage ceremony is the merging of two separate lives into one. That includes each person's spiritual paths. The spiritual beliefs and faith expressions of each person in the relationship will impact the spiritual beliefs and faith expressions of the other.

■ *Describe how you and your mate's religious views and spiritual expressions are similar.*

■ *Describe how you and your mate's religious views and spiritual expressions are different.*

■ *How will the similarities and differences in your religious views and spiritual expressions impact the marriage relationship?*

■ *Do you have any concerns or reservations about merging spiritual paths with your mate? List them.*

■ *If you and your mate have children, which spiritual beliefs and religious practices do you want to ensure are passed on to them?*

Is His Divine Hand on Your Relationship?

DAY FOUR

Is God as active today bringing individuals together for a lifetime relationship as He was in bringing Adam and Eve together? In the Garden, God saw Adam's need for companionship, his need for intimacy, and his need for camaraderie. God fulfilled Adam's needs with Eve.

Couples commonly describe the beginning of their relationship as a chance instance. It was the result of fate, destiny, or the luck of being at the right place at the right time. Some fell in love while others claim it was love at first sight. Could a relationship that results in a lifelong marriage be more than random luck? Could there be a Divine Hand orchestrating the two individuals meeting, growing in love, and sharing a lifetime together?

Couples married for many years often refer to their mate as a gift from God. So how does one tell? Is it necessary to make it to the Golden Anniversary to realize God's involvement in the relationship?

The following questions and statements will help you explore the different seasons of your relationship and look for Divine fingerprints. By replaying the love story that is uniquely yours, you and your mate may discover God has had a much bigger role in the relationship than either of you may have ever thought.

> **When did the two of you meet? What were the circumstances surrounding your first encounter?**

> **Describe what attributes attracted you to your mate.**

> **Describe key milestones in your courtship.**

the Bible says

"And here's a second offense: You fill the place of worship with your whining and sniveling because you don't get what you want from God. Do you know why? Simple. Because God was there as a witness when you spoke your marriage vows to your young bride, and now you've broken those vows, broken the faith-bond with your vowed companion, your covenant wife. God, not you, made marriage. His Spirit inhabits even the smallest details of marriage. And what does He want from marriage? Children of God, that's what. So guard the spirit of marriage within you. Don't cheat on your spouse.

'I hate divorce,' says the God of Israel. God-of-the-Angel-Armies says, 'I hate the violent dismembering of the one flesh of marriage.' So watch yourselves. Don't let your guard down. Don't cheat."
Malachi 2:13-16

When did you realize you wanted to spend the rest of your life with your mate?

Describe how you first began discussing marriage.

When did discussions of marriage move from theory to fact?

Describe how you became engaged.

Were there any instances or periods during your relationship that stand out as extraordinary?

How has this relationship been different from other relationships in which you have been involved?

Do you believe that you and your mate are meant to be together? If yes, why?

Have you ever experienced love like this before?

Replaying Your Love Story

Outline key highlights and lowlights of your love story.

Using your love story as evidence, write a convincing argument on why you and your mate are meant to be together for a lifetime.

In what ways, if any, have you witnessed Divine intervention in your relationship with your mate?

As best as you can determine, is God supportive, neutral, or unsupportive of your decision to marry your mate? Why do you think this?

DAY FIVE

Growing With God as a Couple

the Bible says

"Let the Word of Christ—the Message —have the run of the house. Give it plenty of room in your lives. Instruct and direct one another using good common sense."
Colossians 3:16

the Bible says

"Don't fret or worry. Instead of worrying, pray. Let petitions and praises shape your worries into prayers, letting God know your concerns. Before you know it, a sense of God's wholeness, everything coming together for good, will come and settle you down. It's wonderful what happens when Christ displaces worry at the center of your life."
Philippians 4:6-7

If a couple shares a common faith, they possess a vital and irreplaceable ingredient for their marriage. Affirming one another's spiritual beliefs is not enough. Putting those beliefs into action gives couples a uniquely intimate way to grow their relationship with God and with one another.

It is extremely helpful if couples exercise their faith before children are a part of their life. While some couples wait until kids arrive to begin nurturing the spiritual side of marriage, living a faith-filled life will show any future offspring a genuine religious experience, rather than a well-intentioned religious performance.

The ideas below are simply suggestions to help couples enhance their spiritual life.

Learn About God Together: Couples can learn more about God and their faith by reading Scripture together, attending a Bible study or Sunday school class together, or reading faith-related books. Discussing what they are discovering allows each to learn more.

■ *Currently, how are you as a couple learning about God?*

■ *When married, in what way(s) would you like to learn more about God with your mate?*

Pray Together: There is an old adage that says, "the couple that prays together, stays together." There are a variety of ways to pray together. Couples can pray silently next to one another, pray out loud together, share prayer requests with one another, take a prayer walk together, or journal prayers together.

■ *How often do you and your mate currently pray together? In what way do you currently pray together?*

■ *When married, how would you like to see the practice of prayer lived out with your mate?*

Grow in the Faith Together: By connecting with others, couples can grow in their faith and relationship with God. Finding a faith community (church) is a natural place to find others who want to grow their relationship with God. Attending smaller fellowship groups, reading devotions together, and participating in classes that focus on personal spirituality are all great options for couples.

■ **Currently, how are you as a couple growing in the faith together?**

■ **When married, in what way(s) would you like to grow in the faith with your mate?**

Live Out the Faith Together: Serving in ministry is a rewarding experience for many couples. Utilizing their special gifts and talents, couples can act as a team in special service for a deeper meaning. Participating in outreach events, either locally or internationally, enables couples to live out their faith together.

■ **How are you and your mate currently living out the faith together?**

■ **When married, in what way(s) would you like to live out the faith?**

Concentrating on the spiritual side of your marriage is as important as focusing on the physical, sexual, emotional, and financial sides of your marriage. There are many short-term and long-term benefits that result from couples nurturing the spiritual side of marriage.

Growing spiritual intimacy is not a guarantee that a couple will automatically avoid bad times. But by walking on the spiritual side of marriage, couples set in motion a natural habit and proven spiritual activity that transcends the trials and stresses of life.

Couples who merge their spiritual paths, share religious practices, and grow spiritually together place themselves, their relationship, and their life in the hands of God. They are well positioned to live the *Full Marriage Experience*. What more can a man and woman ask for?

the **Bible** says

"What I'm getting at, friends, is that you should simply keep on doing what you've done from the beginning. When I was living among you, you lived in responsive obedience. Now that I'm separated from you, keep it up. Better yet, redouble your efforts. Be energetic in your life of salvation, reverent and sensitive before God. That energy is God's energy, an energy deep within you, God Himself willing and working at what will give Him the most pleasure."
Philippians 2:12-13

the **Bible** says

"So if you're serious about living this new resurrection life with Christ, act like it. Pursue the things over which Christ presides. Don't shuffle along, eyes to the ground, absorbed with the things right in front of you. Look up, and be alert to what is going on around Christ — that's where the action is. See things from His perspective. Your old life is dead. Your new life, which is your real life — even though invisible to spectators — is with Christ in God. He is your life."
Colossians 3:1-3

worthy **quote**

"After all, love means to serve others for their good. We should have as our goal to make our husband or wife the best Christian possible—in prayer, in ministry, in attitude, in service, in giving, and especially, in loving."
-- Keith Green, *Christian musician*

DAY SIX

Couple Time - Discussion Questions

Take some time to discuss *Walk on the Spiritual Side of Marriage* with one another. Below are questions and statements to spark further discussion and deeper conversation.

■ *Discuss the Faith-Effect on Marriage. What effect will faith have on your marriage?*

■ *Share with one another additional spiritual beliefs (not listed in the chart) that you highly value.*

■ *Do you have spiritual belief differences because of different religious expressions? How will this impact your wedding? Your marriage? Your families? Your future kids?*

■ *Share more about your spiritual journey with one another.*

■ *Are you both willing to yield to one another as you merge spiritual paths, or are you both expecting the other to merge onto your own path?*

■ *How do you feel about merging spiritual paths?*

■ *Do you see God's Divine Hand on your relationship? Why or why not?*

■ *Are you satisfied with how you are growing with God as a couple? Why or why not?*

■ *What changes will need to take place to grow with God as a couple?*

■ *Share how you will walk on the spiritual side of marriage as a couple.*

Marriage Investor Session Notes

DAY SEVEN

Use this space to capture notes, thoughts, and issues that arise while meeting with your Marriage Investor.

Go Deeper

At **www.FullMarriageExperience.com** you will find lists of helpful books and articles, informative web sites, and practical resources related to topics covered in this section.

▪ *Personal Spiritual Growth*
▪ *Spiritual Life in Marriage*
▪ *Inter-faith Issues*
▪ *Questions about Faith and Spirituality*

DAY SEVEN

Section 7

$\mathcal{P}$lan for Your Future Together, Together

Imagine a couple decides to take a yearlong excursion on a large sail-boat. They learn to sail, purchase all the necessary supplies and food for the journey, and acquire a brand new sailboat. They take the time off from work, say their goodbyes to friends and family, and set off for their exciting adventure.

As they launch from the dock and set out from Seattle, they discover they have two different destination plans. She wants to quickly sail down the Pacific coastline to Mexico and spend as much time on the beach as possible. He wants to leisurely sail towards Alaska, stop at every harbor, and learn the historical significance of each port.

This couple had spent so much time sharing a common plan (taking a year off to sail on a boat) that they neglected to discuss their goals (racing down to Mexico for her, leisurely cruising to Alaska for him). Now in the beginning stages of their long trip, they have a huge issue to settle, *"Where are we going?"*

This is a question every couple should ask prior to their wedding, *"Where are we going?"*

Countless couples have married with the misconception that they share common plans for their life together. While their plans may be similar (e.g., to have children), their goals could be completely different (e.g., he wants to have seven children while she wants no more than two children). This can lead to tremendous distress in the relationship and sometimes to a shipwrecked marriage.

This section, **Plan for Your Future Together, Together,** enables couples to gain each other's perspective, discover each other's expectations, and determine each other's priorities in relation to personal and couple goals, family planning, and finances. The intended outcome is to guarantee that when they leave the harbor on their wedding day, they are in full agreement on their destination spot and reach the *Full Marriage Experience.*

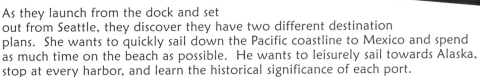

■ *Think about your 50th wedding anniversary. List three things you hope to have accomplished as a couple by that time.*

DAY ONE

Personal Goals & Accomplishments

Having goals is one of the keys to a satisfying life. They can provide motivation, focus, inspiration, purpose, and fulfillment. If goals are unfulfilled or unrealistic, they can create discouragement, frustration, hopelessness, and even depression. It is important to have personal goals, even when an individual gets married.

> *List several goals you have accomplished over your lifetime.*

> *List several personal goals that have yet to be accomplished.*

> *List your personal goals for the following:*

> --**Future marriage:**

> --**Future family:**

> --**Future education:**

> --**Career future:**

> --**Financial future:**

> --**Physical health:**

> --**Spiritual health:**

> *In order, list the top five priorities in your life.*

> 1)

> 2)

> 3)

> 4)

> 5)

> *Finish the statement, "The legacy I hope to leave is ..."*

the Bible says

"A life devoted to things is a dead life, a stump; a God-shaped life is a flourishing tree."
Proverbs 11:28

worthy quote

"Fifty percent of what Billy (Graham) is, is due to his wife, Ruth. She is a strong person in his life, a confidant, a critic of constructive nature, a wise counselor."
-- Harold Lindsell, *friend and colleague of Billy and Ruth Graham.*

the Bible says

"It's in Christ that we find out who we are and what we are living for. Long before we first heard of Christ and got our hopes up, he had his eye on us, had designs on us for glorious living, part of the overall purpose he is working out in everything and everyone."
Ephesians 1:11

Your Mate's Personal Goals

Spend some time reflecting on what you know of your mate's personal goals. Answer the following questions.

List your mate's personal goals for the following:

--Future marriage:

--Future family:

--Future education:

--Career future:

--Financial future:

--Physical health:

--Spiritual health:

Compare your personal goals with your mate's personal goals. What do they seem to have in common or not have in common?

In order, list the top five priorities in your mate's life.

1)

2)

3)

4)

5)

Finish the statement for your mate, "The legacy I hope to leave is ..."

"Living on purpose is the only way to really live. Everything else is just existing."
-- Rick Warren, author of The Purpose-Driven Life

THIS PAGE IS FOR YOU AND YOUR MATE TO WORK ON TOGETHER.

Spend some time discussing the following as a couple.

List your short-term goals (0-5 years) and long-term goals (ten years and more) for the following:

--*Future marriage:*

--*Future family:*

--*Future education:*

--*Career future:*

--*Financial future:*

--*Physical health:*

--*Spiritual health:*

In order, list the top five priorities in your life as a couple:

1)

2)

3)

4)

5)

Do any of your goals or priorities as a couple conflict with either of your personal goals or priorities? If so, which ones?

Finish the statement, "The legacy we hope to leave is ..."

Plotting Your Life Together

Sometimes couples can become so enamored with the fantasy of their wedding day that they neglect to think about the realities of their future married life. Dis-illusionment can hit pretty fast when the dream of being together for a lifetime clashes with day-to-day life.

On your own, envision what a lifetime together will look like. Record your assumptions of what the years may bring—children, career, finances, and major accomplishments. Having a realistic idea of the future together helps expose false perceptions that could disrupt the marriage relationship.

ANNIVERSARIES	Describe where in career-paths you and your mate will be (job, schooling, training).	Describe what your home life will look like (# of kids & ages, childcare).	Describe what your financial status will be like (income, major purchases such as home, car).	Describe what personal and couple accomplish-ments you will have achieved.
ONE YEAR Your age: Mate's age:				
THREE YEAR Your age: Mate's age:				
FIVE YEAR Your age: Mate's age:				
TEN YEAR Your age: Mate's age:				
TWENTY YEAR Your age: Mate's age:				
THIRTY YEAR Your age: Mate's age:				
FORTY YEAR Your age: Mate's age:				
FIFTY YEAR Your age: Mate's age:				

Planning for the Unexpected

Life is unpredictable. People make poor choices. Natural disasters occur sporadically and unexpectedly. Things don't go according to plans. Stuff happens even to the happiest of couples.

To avoid being blindsided by the unexpected, couples must plan for it. Combining a flexible attitude with a knowledge that God has a plan through all circumstances will assure couples that they can overcome most anything life brings their way.

Below is a list of real life events that could occur in anyone's life or marriage. Describe how each would affect you and your mate. Then think about how you would overcome these events. Determine if they will strengthen the marriage, or threaten to weaken it. (For this exercise, events occur after getting married).

LIFE EVENTS	How could this affect you personally?	How could this affect your mate?	Describe steps to overcome this unexpected event.	Will this make your marriage stronger or weaker?
Your mate is laid off from work and is unable to find work in their field.				
The wife unexpectedly gets pregnant on the honeymoon.				
You are unable to conceive children together due to infertility.				
Your mate is diagnosed with cancer and given two years to live.				
You are involved in an accident and paralyzed from the waist down.				
Your 7-year old child is diagnosed with a life threatening disease.				
Your mate has a chemical imbalance that leads to depression and gains 75 pounds.				
A fire destroys your home and all its contents while your family is on vacation.				

Parallel Paths or Different Directions

Now that you have listed out your personal goals and priorities, listed your mate's goals and priorities, mapped out your lifetime together, and briefly planned for the unexpected, you have a better vantage point to view your marriage future. Is it what you expected?

Do you sense from listing you personal goals and priorities that you and your mate are striving for a similar future, or are heading in different directions? Why?

Do you think you and your mate are charting a similar path for your lifetime together? Why or why not?

How will you handle it if the chart for your lifetime together does not play out the way you hope? How will you view your life or your marriage?

What unexpected life events (listed or not) could jeopardize the health and well-being of your marriage?

Do you sense that in the midst of life's trials, you and your mate could work through issues together as a team? Why or why not?

"The happiest times in my life were when my relationships were going well - when I was in love with someone, and someone was loving me. But in my whole life, I haven't met the person I can sustain a relationship with yet. So I'm discontented about that ... I have regrets ... You can't go home with ... You don't sleep with ... You don't get hugged by ... and you don't have children with the Rock and Roll Hall of Fame. I want what everybody else wants: to love and to be loved, and to have a family."
-- Billy Joel, *musician*

"Consider it a sheer gift, friends, when tests and challenges come at you from all sides. You know that under pressure, your faith-life is forced into the open and shows its true colors. So don't try to get out of anything prematurely. Let it do its work so you become mature and well-developed, not deficient in any way."
James 1:2-3

"Any change in the family system — the birth of a baby, the first baby going to school, the last child leaving home, turning forty, an aging and sickly parent, the death of a loved one — challenges even the best of marriages."
-- Michele Weiner-Davis, *author of Divorce Busting*

DAY THREE

worthy
quote

"It doesn't matter how much money you make. It doesn't matter whether you want to buy a starter home or a retirement home, or whether your idea of a big treat is to buy tickets to the movies or tickets on a cruise line. No matter how much money you have, and no matter how much more you earn, there will always be unlimited ways to allocate limited resources."
-- Ron and Judy Blue, *authors of Money Talks and So Can We*

the
Bible
says

"God claims Earth and everything in it, God claims World and all who live on it."
Psalm 24:1

"A devout life does bring wealth, but it's the rich simplicity of being yourself before God. Since we entered the world penniless and will leave it penniless, if we have bread on the table and shoes on our feet, that's enough."
I Timothy 6:6-8

"God can pour on the blessings in astonishing ways so that you're ready for anything and everything, more than just ready to do what needs to be done. As one psalmist puts it, 'He throws caution to the winds, giving to the needy in reckless abandon. His right-living, right-giving ways never run out, never wear out.'

This most generous God who gives seed to the farmer that becomes bread for your meals is more than extravagant with you. He gives you something you can then give away, which grows into full-formed lives, robust in God, wealthy in every way, so that you can be generous in every way, producing with us great praise to God."
II Corinthians 9:8-10

Your Perspective on All Things Money

A major part of life is money; it's rumored to make the world go around.

In opinion surveys asking couples at all seasons of marriage, "what leads to conflict the most in your marriage?" money issues are always cited in the top three responses. A large reason many couples fight about money so often is that these couples don't resolve conflict very well, and money is an issue that comes up on a daily basis.

Another reason for the high rate of conflict with money issues is that couples do not realize that they often approach the topic of money, finances, and budgeting completely differently. This is due to having different priorities for money, different upbringings related to finances, and different opinions on budgeting.

Write a sentence explaining personal values in relation to each of the following financially-related matters.

MONEY IN GENERAL:

LIVING ON A BUDGET:

MAKING MONEY:

SAVING MONEY:

INVESTING MONEY:

ACQUIRING DEBT:

SPENDING MONEY:

PAYING TAXES:

MAKING CONTRIBUTIONS:

A Divine Perspective on Money

In the recorded teachings of Jesus Christ, the subject of money is brought up more than any other topic. This fact shocks a lot of people. Jesus knew many things about finances that most people in His day did not, and many people today need to know.

He did not provide secrets to become a millionaire or stock market investment strategies. The Bible provides guidance to acquire healthy perspectives on money and attain righteous priorities for your money. It also gives stern warnings about money and divine direction on how to use money. Read the Bible verses in the margins. Summarize the verse in a way that can apply to your life.

HEALTHY PERSPECTIVES:
Psalm 24:1 —

I Timothy 6:6-8 —

RIGHTEOUS PRIORITIES:
2 Corinthians 9:8-10 —

Matthew 6:19-20 —

STERN WARNINGS:
I Timothy 6:9-10 —

Proverbs 23:4-5 —

DIVINE DIRECTIVES:
I Timothy 6:17-19 —

Proverbs 3:9 —

As you consider your personal values on financial matters, how similar or different are they from the principles in the Bible passages above?

the Bible says

"'Don't hoard treasure down here where it gets eaten by moths and corroded by rust or —worse!—stolen by burglars. Stockpile treasure in heaven, where it's safe from moth and rust and burglars. It's obvious, isn't it? The place where your treasure is, is the place you will most want to be, and end up being."
Matthew 6:19-20

"Lust for money brings trouble and nothing but trouble. Going down that path, some lose their footing in the faith completely and live to regret it bitterly ever after."
I Timothy 6:9-10

"Don't wear yourself out trying to get rich; restrain yourself! Riches disappear in the blink of an eye; wealth sprouts wings and flies off into the wild blue yonder."
Proverbs 23:4-5

"Tell those rich in this world's wealth to quit being so full of themselves and so obsessed with money, which is here today and gone tomorrow. Tell them to go after God, who piles on all the riches we could ever manage— to do good, to be rich in helping others, to be extravagantly generous. If they do that, they'll build a treasury that will last, gaining life that is truly life."
I Timothy 6:17-19

"Honor God with everything you own; give Him the first and the best. Your barns will burst, your wine vats will brim over."
Proverbs 3:9

DAY FOUR

Assess What You Bring to the Marriage

The following three charts will help couples assess assets, income, and debts and liabilities, individually and together.

Individually fill out the first column of each chart. When together for *Couple Time*, fill in your mate's responses in the second column. In the third column ("COMBINED"), total up the responses from the first two columns. This gives couples a general idea of their financial picture starting from the wedding day. These figures will become your assets, your income, your debts, and your liabilities as husband and wife.

This exercise will help couples form an accurate budget.

TOTAL ASSETS	YOURS	MATE'S	COMBINED
			table one
SAVINGS ACCOUNT			
CERTIFICATE OF DEPOSIT			
STOCK INVESTMENTS			
BOND INVESTMENTS			
RETIREMENT FUNDS			
REAL ESTATE			
CARS			
OTHER			
TOTAL ASSETS			

MONTHLY INCOME   *table two*

	YOURS	MATE'S	COMBINED
GROSS INCOME (JOB 1)			
GROSS INCOME (JOB 2)			
INVESTMENT INCOME			
CHILD SUPPORT			
TRUST INCOME			
RENTAL INCOME			
OTHER INCOME			
OTHER INCOME			
TOTAL INCOME			

DEBTS & LIABILITIES   *table three*

	YOURS	MATE'S	COMBINED
MORTGAGE LOAN			
COLLEGE LOAN			
AUTOMOBILE LOAN			
CREDIT CARD DEBT			
CREDIT CARD DEBT			
CREDIT CARD DEBT			
PERSONAL DEBT			
OTHER			
TOTAL DEBTS & LIABILITIES			

DAY FIVE

Putting a Budget Together

the Bible says

"(Jesus speaking) Listen carefully to what I am saying—and be wary of the shrewd advice that tells you how to get ahead in the world on your own. Giving, not getting, is the way. Generosity begets generosity. Stinginess impoverishes."
Mark 4:24-25

marriage factoid

"Research shows that simply using a credit card for the sake of convenience can make you spend at least thirty percent more than you otherwise would!"

-- Ron Blue

Beginning a marriage with a financial budget in place enables couples to pro-actively alleviate undue stress in their relationship.

The challenges of transitioning from a solo account to a joint account can throw off individuals who are used to making their own priorities, sacrifices, and choices based off their own opinions. That all changes in marriage.

Marriage brings in a whole new level of accountability. Choices impact two people now. Decision-making on purchases tends to take longer and cause more frequent personal sacrifices. What was important as a single person will give way to the priorities of a couple.

At first glance it would seem that singles are giving up their financial freedom. But the economic benefits of being married clearly overshadow the momentary challenges of learning a new method of making financial decisions. There is now the potential for a team approach to making money, saving money, budgeting money, keeping track of money, and finding the best deals in town.

Advice for helping couples put together and keep a budget can be found in numerous practical books and resources. The important first step is to form an initial budget. This should be done with your short-term and long-term financial goals in mind. After that big step is taken, decide who will manage the budget and keep it updated. As a couple, it is important to regularly evaluate your spending habits and financial decisions, but when doing so, commit to making it as conflict-free as possible.

On the next page is a chart to help you identify where your money is going on a monthly basis. Knowing that changes do occur and various expenses change from month-to-month, estimate to the best of your ability. Do this on your own.

When you and your mate get together, record your mate's monthly spending in the second column.

The third column ("OURS") will differ from the previous charts. It <u>will not</u> be a sum total of the previous two columns. Many of the expenses you both have separately will now become one. In the following table discuss the monthly expenses you will have.

MONTHLY EXPENSES   *table four*

	YOURS	MATE'S	OURS
HOUSING EXPENSES *Combine mortgage/rent, property taxes, utilities, insurance, phone, garbage, cable.*			
HEALTHCARE EXPENSES *Combine health insurance, prescription, doctor visits, over-the-counter medicine.*			
TRANSPORTATION EXPENSES *Combine auto payment, insurance, maintenance, parking, transit, gasoline.*			
FOOD EXPENSES *Combine groceries, restaurant, fast food, coffee store, and other meals.*			
HOUSEHOLD EXPENSES *Combine cleaning supplies, home decoration, home improvement, yard care.*			
ENTERTAINMENT EXPENSES *Combine theater, sports events, movie rentals, books/magazines, computer-related.*			
SPECIAL OCCASION EXPENSES *Combine gifts for all occasions (birthdays, anniversaries, holidays), cards, gift supplies.*			
PERSONAL CARE EXPENSES *Combine hair cuts, grooming products, toiletries, beauty supplies.*			
DEBT EXPENSES *Combine credit cards, store cards, and all other debt payments.*			
WARDROBE EXPENSES *Combine work and leisure clothes, shoes, accessories, jewelry.*			
EDUCATION EXPENSES *Combine tuition, books, supplies, college loans, and other educational expenses.*			
CHILD SUPPORT EXPENSES *Combine all child support payments, day care, and child support related expenses.*			
MISCELLANEOUS EXPENSES *Combine all other expenses that do not fit into a previously listed category.*			
TAXES *Combine income taxes, social security, other taxes.*			
CHARITY DONATIONS *Combine church donations, charitable contributions, and other giving.*			
TOTAL MONTHLY EXPENSES			

Adding It All Up

THIS PAGE IS FOR YOU AND YOUR MATE TO WORK ON TOGETHER.

Now that you and your mate have completely combined and determined your assets, your income, your debts and liabilities, and your monthly expenditures, you possess a clear view of the new financial picture that begins on your wedding day.

From the previous pages, add up the categories and fill in the following:

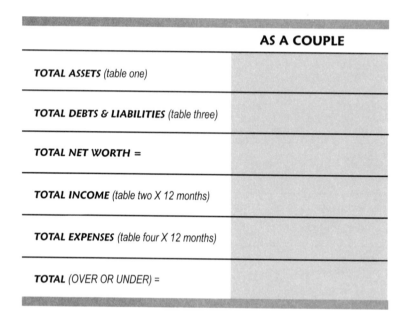

	AS A COUPLE
TOTAL ASSETS (table one)	
TOTAL DEBTS & LIABILITIES (table three)	
TOTAL NET WORTH =	
TOTAL INCOME (table two X 12 months)	
TOTAL EXPENSES (table four X 12 months)	
TOTAL (OVER OR UNDER) =	

▌ *How will combining assets, and debts and liabilities affect your relationship?*

▌ *How will combining incomes and utilizing a budget affect your relationship?*

Couple Time - Discussion Questions

Compare your responses from all the charts in **Plan for Your Future Together, Together** with one another.   Remember to write down your mate's responses in the remaining columns.   There are also a couple of exercises for you to do as a couple.

The questions and statements below are to spark further conversation and discussion.

■ *Compare your personal goals and priorities. How common are your goals?*

■ *Create goals and priorities for your marriage that will allow you to step into marriage with purpose.*

■ *Share stories of couples you know who have gone through great trials. Did their marriages survive? Why?*

■ *Are there additional "unexpected" events that could impact your marriage that concern you?*

■ *Talk about how your parents shaped your perspectives on money, finances, and budgeting.*

■ *As you look at your combined assets, what new issues arise in your relationship?*

■ *How will your lifestyle change as you combine incomes?*

■ *Share concerns you have as you add up your combined debt load.*

DAY SEVEN

Marriage Investor Session Notes

Use this space to capture notes, thoughts, and issues that arise while meeting with your Marriage Investor.

Go Deeper

At **www.FullMarriageExperience.com** you will find lists of helpful books and articles, informative web sites, and practical resources related to topics covered in this section.

- *Personal & Couple Goals*
- *Finding Purpose in Life*
- *Overcoming Challenges*
- *Financial Issues*
- *Budgeting*

Section 8

Prepare the Marriage Bed for a Lifetime of Pleasure

Sex is everywhere. And it seems to have reached a saturation level in today's society. It is talked about in popular songs, discussed on television programs, portrayed in the movies, and displayed on magazine covers. The unconventional theories from the sixties' sexual revolution have become the mainstream attitudes of the 21st century.

At an extremely permissive time in history and with unlimited access to information through different venues, it would seem that the people's sexual issues of yesteryear would have been addressed and alleviated.

Society's daily infatuation with all things sex has exposed a greater personal confusion surrounding sex, intimacy, and romance both inside and outside of marriage. Rates of young people contracting sexually transmitted diseases are high, the percentage of women having children without the security of marriage is higher, and the numbers of men and women with sexual dysfunctions have climbed to all-time highs.

Yet through the fog of confusion, disillusionment, and ignorance shines truth. The Author of Marriage is also the Creator of Sex.

And just as God provides greater insights on marriage matters, He reveals His intentions for sex in the Scriptures. He desires for a husband and wife to foster a long-term, healthy sex life. Mastering His principles for the bedroom gives couples a much better chance to live the *Full Marriage Experience*.

This section, **Prepare the Marriage Bed for a Lifetime of Pleasure**, details God's intended purposes for sex in marriage, provides practical insight to foster a healthy, vibrant sex life, and brings light to obstacles couples can overcome to grow sexually throughout their marriage.

Reflecting over your lifetime, from whom have you received the bulk of your information and insight on sexual matters? Were they accurate? Were they informative? Were they helpful?

DAY ONE

God's Intention for Sex:
Sex is to be between a man and woman within the marriage relationship to unify and celebrate their love, deepen intimacy in a uniquely pleasurable way that reveres and glorifies God, and provide an opportunity to create life.

"As an apricot tree stands out in the forest, my lover stands above the young men in town. All I want is to sit in his shade, to taste and savor his delicious love. He took me home with him for a festive meal, but his eyes feasted on me!"
Song of Solomon 2:3-4

"My lover is mine, and I am his. Nightly he strolls in our garden, delighting in the flowers until dawn breathes its light and night slips away. Turn to me, dear lover. Come like a gazelle. Leap like a wild stag on delectable mountains."
Song of Solomon 2:16-17

"Oh, let me warn you, sisters in Jerusalem, by the gazelles, yes, by all the wild deer: Don't excite love, don't stir it up, until the time is ripe — and you're ready."
Song of Solomon 3:5

"Come and look, sisters in Jerusalem. Oh, sisters of Zion, don't miss this! My King-Lover, dressed and garlanded for his wedding, his heart full, bursting with joy!"
Song of Solomon 3:11

"A garden fountain, sparkling and splashing, fed by spring waters from the Lebanon mountains. Wake up, North Wind, get moving, South Wind! Breathe on my garden, fill the air with spice fragrance. Oh, let my lover enter his garden! Yes, let him eat the fine, ripe fruits."
Song of Solomon 4:15-16

"I went to my garden, dear friend, best lover! I breathed the sweet fragrance. I ate the fruit and honey, I drank the nectar and wine. Celebrate with me, friends! Raise your glasses — 'To life! To love!'"
Song of Solomon 5:1

"I am my lover's. I'm all he wants. I'm all the world to him!"
Song of Solomon 7:10

God's Ideals on Intimate Relationships

Marriage is where sex, intimacy, and romance reside. It is within marriage that focused passion and healthy romance collide.

God intends sex to be between a man and woman within the marriage relationship to unify and celebrate their love, deepen intimacy in a uniquely pleasurable way that reveres and glorifies God, and provide an opportunity to create life.

The following Scriptural insights will build upon this premise.

-- A Healthy Model for the Natural Progression of an Intimate Relationship—Song of Solomon 1:1—8:14

Hailed as one of the most romantic pieces of ancient literature, Song of Solomon captures the intimate details and feelings in the story of a young king and a young maiden falling in love, marrying one another, and growing in that love. This poetic piece creates an incredible picture of experiencing love in all of its majesty, passion, and purity.

The entire book of Song of Solomon acts as a healthy model for the natural progression for an intimate relationship that receives God's approval and endorsement. Song of Solomon can be outlined in this way:
-- First Glances, Impressions, and Encounter (1:2-14)
-- A Growing Courtship (1:15-2:7)
-- An Adoring Engagement (2:8-3:5)
-- The Majestic Wedding Day (3:6-11)
-- Love Unleashed on the Wedding Night (4:1-5:1)
-- Love Unfolding and Maturing through Experiences (5:2-8:14)

(Read the highlight verses in the sidebar or the entire story in the Bible.)

The poetic imagery through this account displays the lover's deep respect, anticipation, and admiration for the fullness of love. The lovers advance in their relationship, intensify in their love, and fully express their love by uniting sexually on their wedding night.

On their first night as husband and wife, the use of analogies display the euphoric, majestic, and fresh beginnings of their physical life together. The *"sealed fountain"* becomes *"a well of flowing water."* The *"locked up"* garden becomes unlocked for each lover to enter into. This occurs with the full endorsement of God, pleased how these two can fully enjoy the sanctuary of deep intimacy He has created (*"Eat, O friends, and drink; drink your fill, O Lovers"*).

How does your relationship relate to the story of the two lovers?

Esteeming Sex in the City

Society has a staked interest in the sex lives of people. When a society has no boundaries or sets too low a value on sex, the results cause a form of sexual chaos. Promiscuity increases, risky behavior increases, stable relationships falter, and the society's most vulnerable fall victim to the predatory nature of uninhibited sexual appetites.

History reveals a few societies that have overburdened boundaries around sex, robbing married couples of the joy and pleasure God intends it to bring. God provides a societal standard for the good of all people. No one is harmed, no one is overburdened, and society is freed from carrying the burdensome weight of irresponsible choices.

-- A Call to Revere the Act of Marriage — Hebrews 13:4
God proclaims here that all people should hold the marriage relationship in high esteem. But not only should society honor marriage, they are to revere the act of marriage (sex) by reserving it for marriage.

-- A Call to Sexual Integrity — I Thessalonians 4:1-8
Living in a culture with conflicting teachings and attitudes regarding sex breeds broad confusion and limitless pain. Valueless instruction devalues God's original intentions for His sacred creation. This passage provides insight on a call to sexual integrity that heightens people's understanding to acquire healthy attitudes about sex and follow it up with action that values God's intent for sex.

> -- *God Desires People to be Virtuous in Their Actions* (4:3)
> -- *Destructive Sexual Activity Exists and Must be Avoided* (4:3)
> -- *With God, People Can Control Their Sexual Behavior* (4:4)
> -- *People Must Learn to Restrain Their Sexual Appetite* (4:4-5)
> -- *Valuing Other People is Important to God* (4:6)
> -- *A Righteous Lifestyle is Possible Through God* (4:7-8)

If sex is such a wonderful gift from God, why do you think God reserved sex exclusively for marriage?

In what ways do you revere marriage and the act of marriage?

What values or system of beliefs have shaped your attitudes and behavior towards sex?

the Bible says

"Honor marriage, and guard the sacredness of sexual intimacy between wife and husband. God draws a firm line against casual and illicit sex."
Hebrews 13:4

"One final word, friends. We ask you—urge is more like it—that you keep on doing what we told you to do to please God, not in a dogged religious plod, but in a living, spirited dance. You know the guidelines we laid out for you from the Master Jesus. God wants you to live a pure life.

Keep yourselves from sexual promiscuity. Learn to appreciate and give dignity to your body, not abusing it, as is so common among those who know nothing of God.

Don't run roughshod over the concerns of your brothers and sisters. Their concerns are God's concerns, and He will take care of them. We've warned you about this before. God hasn't invited us into a disorderly, unkempt life but into something holy and beautiful—as beautiful on the inside as the outside.

If you disregard this advice, you're not offending your neighbors; you're rejecting God, who is making you a gift of His Holy Spirit."
I Thessalonians 4:1-8

DAY TWO

The Call to Celebrate Sex for Life

"Do you know the saying, 'Drink from your own rain barrel, draw water from your own spring-fed well'? It's true. Otherwise, you may one day come home and find your barrel empty and your well polluted.

Your spring water is for you and you only, not to be passed around among strangers. Bless your fresh-flowing fountain! Enjoy the wife you married as a young man! Lovely as an angel, beautiful as a rose — don't ever quit taking delight in her body. Never take her love for granted! Why would you trade enduring intimacies for cheap thrills with a whore? For dalliance with a promiscuous stranger?"
Proverbs 5:15-19

"Now, getting down to the questions you asked in your letter to me. First, is it a good thing to have sexual relations?

Certainly—but only within a certain context. It's good for a man to have a wife, and for a woman to have a husband. Sexual drives are strong, but marriage is strong enough to contain them and provide for a balanced and fulfilling sexual life in a world of sexual disorder. The marriage bed must be a place of mutuality—the husband seeking to satisfy his wife, the wife seeking to satisfy her husband. Marriage is not a place to 'stand up for your rights.' Marriage is a decision to serve the other, whether in bed or out. Abstaining from sex is permissible for a period of time if you both agree to it, and if it's for the purposes of prayer and fasting—but only for such times. Then come back together again. Satan has an ingenious way of tempting us when we least expect it. I'm not, understand, commanding these periods of abstinence —only providing my best counsel if you should choose them."
I Corinthians 7:1-6

"God blessed them: 'Prosper! Reproduce! Fill Earth! Take charge!'"
Genesis 1:28

God wants married couples to fully enjoy and celebrate in the act of marriage. He provides insights to ensure that the best interests of husband, wife, and society are protected.

-- The Call to Healthy Sexual Relations — Proverbs 5:15-19

The verses in this chapter give a fervent warning on the shallowness and destructive nature of allowing oneself to sexually venture outside of marriage. This section of Proverbs is a strong encouragement for husbands and wives to direct any and all of their spousal affections, sensual attentions, sexual desires, and physical ambitions within their marriage relationship.

-- *Keep Sexual Expressions Inside the Marriage (5:15)*
-- *Avoid All Corruptive Sexual Behavior (5:16-17)*
-- *Adore Your Spouse (5:18)*
-- *Pleasure in Your Spouse (5:19-20)*

-- The Call to Fulfilling One Another's Needs — I Corinthians 7:1-6

A man and a woman both possess a sex drive and have physical longings. Within marriage, the attitude should be focused on fulfilling the sexual needs of one's spouse, rather than focusing solely on one's own cravings and desires.

-- *Marriage Stabilizes Sex (7:2)*
-- *Sexual Responsibility Falls on Both Husband & Wife (7:3)*
-- *The Husband & Wife Belong to Each Other (7:4)*
-- *Avoid Sexual Power Trips (7:5)*
-- *Abstinence is Okay for Temporary Spiritual Moments (7:5)*
-- *A Sexual Famine Can Lead to Destruction (7:5)*
-- *This Instruction is Well Advised (7:6)*

-- The Call to Create Life — Genesis 1:28

Every time a man and woman unite in the sex act, the potential for creating life exists. The sperm and the egg do not look for wedding rings, check personal identification, or make reference calls for the responsibility levels of the sexually-engaging participants.

God has established marriage to be the relationship in which this ability to create new life is not only appropriate, but endorsed. No other type of relationship is given the mandate to create life, produce children, and raise them. It is an awesome responsibility given to those who have already determined to be together for life.

How will you celebrate sex in your marriage?

■ *What are your plans to keep your sexual relations healthy?*

■ *What will you do to fulfill the sexual needs of your mate?*

■ *How will the potential to create life affect your sex life? Is there a method of birth control the two of you plan to use?*

■ *How long do you want to be married before you and your mate create life?*

"Sex is like a river – it is a good and wonderful blessing when kept within its proper channel. A river that overflows its banks is a dangerous thing ... What are the God-created banks for sex? One man and one woman in marriage for life."
-- Richard Foster, *author of Celebration of Discipline*

"As husband and wife come together, they form a family, the core institution of human society – the training ground, in fact, for all other social institutions. Human sexuality is not designed only as a source of pleasure or a means of expressing affection. It was designed as a powerful bond between husband and wife in order to form a secure, stable environment for raising vulnerable children to adulthood."
-- Chuck Colson, *author*

Discovering How to Love & Be Loved

DAY THREE

Love can be shown in a number of different ways. It can be received in a number of different ways too. Just because love in shown and received doesn't mean couples have connected emotionally.

The Anatomy of Love is six distinct ways partners demonstrate and live out love. Every person responds differently to the *Anatomy of Love;* some produce a greater sense of feeling loved, while others don't have as great an impact.   Learning how a mate wants to be shown love helps couples actively love their mate so they feel loved.

During married life, if a spouse is not feeling connected to their mate, it may be that their *Anatomy of Love* is being neglected.

Every married couple must discover their unique combination of how to love and be loved to ensure the husband and wife feel loved.

Below is the *Anatomy of Love*. After reading through the list of descriptions, rank your *Anatomy of Love* (yourself only) on the chart below in numerical order (1-6) from most meaningful (6) to least meaningful (1). During *Couple Time*, share answers with your mate.

ANATOMY OF LOVE

-- Mouth
Love is shown by kind words, encouraging statements, compliments, and words of affirmation.

-- Ears
Love is shown through meaningful conversation, undivided attention while talking, and speaking beyond the surface level.

-- Body
Love is demonstrated through physical touch, sensual touches, kisses, cuddling, holding hands, stroking one another, and sex.

-- Presence
Love is shown by spending time together, being around one another, having quality time together, and doing something together.

-- Hands
Love is shown by acts of service, doing things for the other that they would appreciate.

-- Heart
Love is demonstrated by giving gifts, meaningful and thoughtful gifts that are made, bought, or found.

	ME on ME	MATE on MATE
MOUTH		
EARS		
BODY		
PRESENCE		
HANDS		
HEART		

In what ways and how often does your mate show you love with your highest Anatomy of Love?

Cultivating a Lifelong Sex Life

Growing a healthy, vibrant sex life over the entire lifetime of a marriage takes intentionality and teamwork. Excelling in the marriage bed demands that couples possess helpful perspectives to growing their love life, and healthy approaches to fostering sexual fusion.

HELPFUL PERSPECTIVES TO GROWING YOUR LOVE LIFE

-- Realize Men & Women Differ in this Area Too
Men and women approach sex differently, react to sex differently, and respond to sex differently. Men are more visually stimulated, progress in passion rather rapidly, and have a shorter, more intensive climax. Women tend to be stimulated by the feelings of security in the relationship, progress more slowly than men, and have longer, more drawn out (and perhaps multiple) orgasms. What a husband and wife share in common is a desire for making love.

-- Take Time for Discovery
There is a lot more to good sex than a romantic atmosphere. In many cases, a spouse's initial assumptions on what pleasures their mate tend to be incorrect. Explore new ways of sexual expression and then plan to discuss later what worked and what didn't. Exploratory lovemaking should not be rushed. Use extreme patience. Over time, increased sexual harmony will occur more regularly and more frequently.

-- Communicate In & Out of the Bedroom
In order for the sex life of a couple to grow, they must talk about it. Avoid taking things personally, and as much as possible, maintain conflict-free discussions. Talk about events in the bedroom at appropriate times and avoid detailed remarks with others on this topic. This is a highly sensitive and intimate part of marriage that will not profit from outside consensus on personal performance issues.

-- View the Whole Day as Foreplay
Take a wholistic approach to lovemaking. Take the entire day to prepare the mental, emotional, and spiritual needs of each other and make the marriage bed the place where those efforts culminate. Talking, touching, and flirting over the course of a day heightens the anticipation levels for that sacred time together.

marriage factoid

"Men told us that they think about sex often - more than half (54%) said they have erotic thoughts every day or several times a day ...(w)omen, in contrast, more often (67%) report that they think about sex a few times a week to a few time a month."

-- Sex in America

worthy quote

"It is very important for all couples to find ways to protect their privacy, to cherish their sexual relationship, to guard it fiercely. A richly rewarding and stable sex life is not just a fringe benefit; it is the central task of marriage. In a good marriage, sex and love are inseparable. Sex serves a very serious function in maintaining both the quality and stability of the relationship, replenishing emotional reserves, and strengthening the marital bond."
-- Judith Wallerstein, author of The Legacy of Divorce

worthy quote

"Seems to me the basic conflict between men and women, sexually, is that men are like firemen. To us, sex is an emergency, and no matter what we're doing we can be ready in two minutes. Women, on the other hand, are like fire. They're very exciting, but the conditions have to be exactly right for it to occur."
-- Jerry Seinfeld, comedian

HELPFUL PERSPECTIVES TO GROWING YOUR LOVE LIFE continued

-- Focus on Satisfying the Other

Selfishness during sexual encounters with one another is a guarantee that one of the participants will walk away dissatisfied and frustrated from the experience. The more one-sided satisfaction occurs, the less interested the other mate will be in sexually uniting. To counter this, a spouse should enter the sexual arena with one purpose in mind, to bring pleasure to their mate. If both spouses are taking this approach to sex, both are more likely to experience satisfaction.

-- Relax & Avoid Stressing about It

Because sexual expression is so deeply intimate and personal, it can be a breeding ground for insecurity and stress. Avoid placing too many unrealistic or inappropriate expectations on yourself or your mate. It can breed sexual dysfunction such as impotency, inability to orgasm, and other distractions. Relax! By being open about issues of perfor-mance and activity, the marriage bed becomes a stress-free zone, in more ways than one.

-- Ask Questions

If in doubt, ask questions. Doctors can be a great source of informa-tion on all kinds of issues related to sex. From offering suggestions on hygiene and family planning, to providing help on sexual dysfunctions and health issues, they can be a great source of information. Also, many books on sex have been written to help provide answers to couples' questions.

-- Remember God

God created sex for the sake of married couples and takes joy in their ability to fully enjoy it. By keeping the sex life positive and seeking to revere God in the marriage bed, the physical union will always carry with it much more significant meaning. See it as a form of worship to God.

Which perspectives from this section are new information for you?

Which perspectives from this section seem most helpful to you?

■ *Which perspectives will seem most helpful to your mate?*

■ *How will the two of you apply those most helpful perspectives to your love life?*

■ *List any of the perspectives with which you are uncomfortable with.*

■ *What love-life related issues are causing you stress?*

"I'm not saying sex is everything. If you have a good sexual relationship, it registers about ten percent on the 'important scale' – meaning it makes up about ten percent of what's important in the relationship. But if you do not have a good sexual relationship, that registers about ninety percent on the 'important scale.' A good sexual relationship can make you feel more relaxed, accepted, and more involved with your partner. But if you life together is devoid of sex, then the issue becomes a gigantic focus of the relationship."
-- **Dr. Phil McGraw,** host of Dr. Phil television program

■ *To whom can you turn for more information and/or help with your love-life issues?*

■ *How will you "remember God" when approaching the marriage bed?*

HEALTHY APPROACHES TO FOSTER SEXUAL FUSION

Keeping sexual experiences from developing into predictable physical workout routines takes intentional effort on behalf of the couple. Listed below are some ideas to keep variety and freshness in the act of marriage.

-- *Plan & Unplan Times Together*
Life is busy and can crowd out many of the most necessary and enjoyable things in life, sex included. Couples who lead busy lives can do themselves a favor by safeguarding their sex life. Agreeing to certain times and days each week for lovemaking allows both partners to prepare for and protect those special times. On the flipside, spontaneity is crucial to keeping things spicy. A combination of planned and unplanned times together enable regular sex activity as well as impulsive escapades.

-- *Take Turns Playing Follow the Leader*
Men tend to initiate sex. Women more often respond. Make times where those roles switch. It can be a source of great stimulation as well as a confidence booster for both the husband and the wife.

-- *Feast on an Assortment of Sexual Excursions*
Having sex has been equated to eating meals. Due to a variety of reasons, every meal cannot be fast food, nor can every meal be a nine-course feast. But by mixing up trips through the drive-thru with the trips to the fancy restaurant, combined with eating homemade meals every mealtime experience can be more enjoyable.

Variety has that kind of power in the bedroom as well. There are times for "quickies" (fast, intense times of mutual passion). There are times for "nights of passion" (highly romantic, extensive evenings of pleasure). There is need for "utility sex" (times for release or to relieve stress). There is also a need for "regular lovemaking" (low maintenance and regular times together). A combination of all four types of sexual excursions keep a healthy balance of variety that makes every experience more enjoyable.

How will you and your mate foster sexual fusion in your married life?

Getting Off to a Fresh Start

The lack of a cohesive cultural vision for sex and a missing reverence for marriage in society has fueled the sexual permissiveness of modern times. This has led us to become a sexually broken nation.

Studies reveal that far too many women and men have experienced sexual trauma of some sort at the hands of a trusted adult, a stranger, or peer. Surveys of adults show that many became sexually active too early, too often, and with too many regrets. The pain, consequences, and aftermath of a sexual excursion can last for years after the incident.

The topic of sex can bring to the surface feelings and emotions that may not have been properly dealt with for healing to take place. They may have been buried, denied, or temporarily set aside. If not handled completely, they can manifest themselves into the life of the marriage.

Let the healing begin now! You may need God's forgiveness on some matters. Perhaps you need to ask your mate for forgiveness. Maybe you need to seek a third party for help. Let God provide the necessary healing to enable you to overcome the pain of the past. You are invited to pray by yourself and possibly as a couple (if it is appropriate) and let God take any and all anxiety away from you.

Now is the time to make a fresh start. Even though it is sometimes difficult and painful to face issues of the past (or present), it is necessary for the sake of your future marriage relationship. If you and your mate will be discussing these matters, focus on the feelings and avoid getting into greater detail than is necessary. There is no need for you to carry guilt or shame any longer.

Are there any personal barriers in relation to sex that you fear could be an obstacle to your love life? If so, please list.

Are there any past experiences that need to be dealt with now to prevent them from being barriers to growing intimacy in your marriage? If so, please list.

Are there any damaging influences that could potentially jeopardize the well being of your married sex life? If so, please list.

worthy **quote**

"Marriage and family help establish rules for sexual conduct. Throughout all time, societies have known that sex is not only the most powerful of human passions but an activity whose repercussions can be hugely destructive, wrecking human lives and inflicting wounds that can easily last a lifetime. That is why all societies have undertaken to guide sexuality by means of ritual and law."
-- **William J. Bennett,** author of The Book of Virtues

the **Bible** says

"If we claim that we're free of sin, we're only fooling ourselves. A claim like that is errant nonsense. On the other hand, if we admit our sins—make a clean breast of them—He won't let us down; He'll be true to Himself. He'll forgive our sins and purge us of all wrongdoing."
1 John 1:8-9

the **Bible** says

"Live carefree before God; He is most careful with you."
1 Peter 5:7

DAY SIX | Couple Time - Discussion Questions

Discuss **Prepare the Marriage Bed for a Lifetime of Pleasure** with one another. Consider the following as you talk about this section.

▢ *Share your responses to questions on the Scriptural insights on relationships, sex, and marriage.*

▢ *How similar or different is your Anatomy of Love?*

▢ *What will you do to love each other with your highest ranked Anatomy of Love?*

▢ *How will you grow your love life?*

▢ *Determine together what helpful perspectives you as a couple will apply to grow your love life.*

▢ *How will you foster sexual fusion in your love life?*

▢ *Are there any obstacles in your personal lives that could be a barrier to growing sexual intimacy within your marriage?*

▢ *How will you overcome any obstacles that could thwart the growth in your love life?*

Marriage Investor Session Notes

Use this space to capture notes, thoughts, and issues that arise while meeting with your Marriage Investor.

Go Deeper

At **www.FullMarriageExperience.com** you will find lists of helpful books and articles, informative web sites, and practical resources related to topics covered in this section.

- *Romance*
- *Love*
- *Sexual Issues*
- *Lovemaking*

Sources

Before "I Do" is filled with material aimed to help couples prepare for the *Full Marriage Experience*. Because the author relied on numerous resources to create this book, as much as possible, the author attempts to give credit where credit is due. Whether the information is a direct citation or was inspired by the original writings, the primary source, person, or organization that inspired the material is cited in this section. Although the author and publisher have made every effort to ensure the accuracy and completeness of information contained in this book, we assume no responsibility for errors, inaccuracies, omissions, or any inconsistency herein. Any slights of people, places, or organizations are unintended.

Because most readers find footnote numbers disruptive and distracting, the sources are listed by section, page number, and area on page.

Section ONE

1-6 Marriage Factoid (MF): Kreider, Rose M. and Jason M. Fields. *"Number, Timing, and Duration of Marriages and Divorces: 1996."* U.S. Census Bureau, Issued February 2002. Maher, Bridget (editor). *The Family Portrait: A Compilation of Data, Research and Public Opinion on the Family*, p. 3. The Family Research Council, Washington DC, 2002. Stanley, Scott M. *"What Really is the Divorce Rate?"* www.prepinc.com.

1-8 Worthy Quote (WQ): Margaret Thatcher quote found at www.familyweek.info.

1-9 WQ: Dietrich Bonhoeffer quote from Bethge, Eberhard (editor) *Letters & Papers from Prison*, *"A Wedding Sermon from a Prison Cell,"* p.43. Collier Books, New York, 1972.

1-9 WQ: Stanton, Glenn T. *Why Marriage Matters: Reasons to Believe in Marriage in a Postmodern Society*, p. 44. Pinion Press, Colorado Springs, Colorado, 1997.

1-10 WQ: Popenoe, David and Barbara Dafoe Whitehead. *The State of Our Unions - 2003: The Social Health of Marriage in America*, p.4. The National Marriage Project, Piscataway, New Jersey, 2003.

1-10 WQ: Author unknown. From a posting on the Internet.

1-12 - 1-14 Section Body (SB): *Five-Dimensional Love* inspired by Wheat, Ed. *Staying in Love for a Lifetime*, p. 47-51. Inspirational Press, New York, 1994.

1-12 WQ: Anonymous quote from Canfield, Jack and Mark Victor Hansen. *A 5th Portion of Chicken Soup for the Soul: 101 Stories to Open the Heart and Rekindle the Spirit*, p. 81. Health Communications, Inc., Deerfield Beach, Florida, 1998.

1-15 MF: Ibid. Maher, p. 5.

1-17 MF: List of couples and their length of marriage from www.entertainment.msn.com. Giantis, Kat. *"When the Vow Breaks: We dissect the top 10 shortest celebrity marriages,"* MSN Entertainment.

1-17 WQ: Governor Frank Keating quote from Anderson, Katherine, Don Browning and Brian Boyers (editors). *Marriage—Just a Piece of Paper?*, p. 337. William B. Eerdmans Publishing Company, 2002.

1-18 WQ: Colson, Charles and Nancy Pearcey. *How Now Shall We Live?* p. 320. Tyndale House Publishers, Inc., Wheaton, Illinois, 1999.

1-19 WQ: Dietrich Bonhoeffer quote from Bethge, *Letters & Papers from Prison*, p. 42.

1-20 WQ: George Eliot quote from Bennett, William J. *The Broken Hearth*, p. 186. Doubleday, New York, 2001.

Section TWO

2-24 WQ: Anonymous quotes found at www.thinkexist.com/quotations/men_and_women.html *"Men and Women quotes."* ThinkExist.com Quotations Online.

2-25 WQ: Natalie Wood quote found at www.thinkexist.com/quotations/men_and_women.html *"Men and Women quotes."* ThinkExist.com Quotations Online.

2-25 WQ: Rocky Balboa quote found at www.smartmarriages.com/marrige.quotes.html. *"Marriage quotes."* Coalition for Marriage, Family and Couples Education.

2-25 WQ: Russell Kelfer poem from Warren, Rick. *The Purpose Driven Life*, p. 25-26. Zondervan, Grand Rapids, Michigan, 2002.

2-27 WQ: Ibid. Bennett, p. 185.

2-27 WQ: Leo Tolstoy quote found at www.smartmarriages.com/marriage.quotes.html. *"Marriage quotes."* Coalition for Marriage, Family and Couples Education.

2-30 WQ: Sam Keen quote found at www.samkeen.com/fontsize2bwonderingsbfontp/. *"Quotes, Quarks and Fragments."* Sam Keen.

2-34 WQ: Dave Barry quote found at www.thinkexist.com/quotations/men_and_women.html *"Men and Women quotes."* ThinkExist.com Quotations Online.

2-34 WQ: Zig Ziglar quote found at www.smartmarriages.com/marriage.quotes.html. *"Marriage quotes."* Coalition for Marriage, Family and Couples Education.

2-35 WQ: Hybels, Bill. *Honest to God?*, p. 68. Zondervan Books, Grand Rapids, Michigan, 1990.

Section THREE

3-40 MF: Fields, Jason. *"Children's Living Arrangements and Characteristics: March 2002."* *Current Population Reports*, p. 20-547. U.S. Census Bureau, Washington DC, 2003.

3-41 WQ: Unknown quote found at www.smartmarriages.com/marriage.quotes.html. *"Marriage quotes."* Coalition for Marriage, Family and Couples Education.

3-42 SB: *Three Types of Couple Identities* inspired by Parrott, Les and Leslie Parrott. *Saving Your Marriage Before It Starts*, p. 26-28. Zondervan Publishing House, Grand Rapids, Michigan, 1995.

3-42 WQ: Rose Kennedy quote found at www.thinkexist.com/quotations/men_and_women.html *"Men and Women quotes."* ThinkExist.com Quotations Online.

3-42 WQ: Pearl S. Buck quote found at www.thinkexist.com/quotations/men_and_women.html *"Men and Women quotes."* ThinkExist.com Quotations Online.

3-43 WQ: Ibid. Bennett, p. 186-187.

3-44 WQ: Martin Luther King, Jr. quote from Eubanks, Steve. *Quotable King: Words of Wisdom, Inspiration, and Freedom by and about Dr. Martin Luther King, Jr.*, p. 25. TowleHouse Publishing, Nashville, Tennessee, 2002.

3-46-48 SB: *God's Divine Reminders for Husbands and God's Divine Reminders for Wives* inspired by Wheat, *Staying in Love for a Lifetime*, p. 309-319, 321-336.

3-49 SB: *Expectations* inspired by Stanley, Scott, Daniel Trathen, Savanna McCain and Milt Bryan. *A Lasting Promise: A Christian Guide to Fighting For Your Marriage*, p. 138-150. Jossey-Bass Publishers, San Francisco, 1998.

3-50 WQ: Carl Whitaker quote found at www.smartmarriages.com/marriage.quotes.html. *"Marriage quotes."* Coalition for Marriage, Family and Couples Education.

3-50 WQ: George Eliot quote found at found at www.smartmarriages.com/marriage.quotes.html. *"Marriage quotes".* Coalition for Marriage, Family and Couples Education.

3-51 WQ: Dr. Joyce Brothers quote found at www.thinkexist.com/quotations/men_and_women.html *"Men and Women quotes."* ThinkExist.com Quotations Online.

3-51 WQ: Lewis, C.S. *The Joyful Christian: 127 Readings*, p. 198-199. Macmillan Publishing, New York, 1977.

Section FOUR

4-56–4-58 SB: *Fighting Games* adapted from Stanley, et al. *A Lasting Promise*, p.29-43.

4-56 MF: Stanley, Scott M. and Howard J. Markman. *"Facts About Marital Distress and Divorce,"* University of Denver and PREP, Inc.

4-58 MF: Stanley, Scott M. and Howard J. Markman. *Marriage in the 90's: A Nationwide Random Survey.* PREP, Inc., Denver, Colorado, 1997.

4-61 SB: *Mixed Messages* section adapted from Stanley, et al. *A Lasting Promise*, p. 38-39. Marriage Encounter weekend conducted by Life-Trac Family Ministries, Leavenoworth, Washington, November 1998. The Christian PREP Training Workshop conducted by Dr. Scott Stanley, Salem Oregon, April 23, 1999.

4-59 WQ: Anonymous quote found at www.smartmarriages.com/marriage.quotes.html. *"Marriage quotes."* Coalition for Marriage, Family and Couples Education.

4-59 WQ: Robert Louis Stevenson quote found at www.smartmarriages.com/marriage.quotes.html. *"Marriage quotes."* Coalition for Marriage, Family and Couples Education.

4-60 WQ: Anonymous quote found at www.thinkexist.com/quotations/men_and_women.html *"Men and Women quotes."* ThinkExist.com Quotations Online.

4-60 WQ: Helen Rowland quote found at www.thinkexist.com/quotations/men_and_women.html *"Men and Women quotes."* ThinkExist.com Quotations Online.

4-62 SB: *XYZ Statement* from Parrott and Parrott, *Saving Your Marriage Before It Starts*, p. 123. Original source is Gottman, John Mordecai, Cliff Notarius, Jonni Gonso, Howard Markman. *A Couples Guide to Communication.* Research Press, Illinois, 1976.

4-62 MF: Center for Marriage and Family—Creighton University. *Time, Sex and Money: The First Five Years of Marriage.* p. 41. Center for Marriage and Family—Creighton University, Omaha, Nebraska, 2000.

4-62 WQ: Baumgardner, Julie. *"Irreconcilable Differences,"* Family E-Flash by Families Northwest, June 12, 2002.

4-62 SB: *Speaker-Listener Technique* adapted from Stanley, et al. *A Lasting Promise*, p. 58-65.

4-63 WQ: Paul Tillich quote found at www.smartmarriages.com/marriage.quotes.html. *"Marriage quotes."* Coalition for Marriage, Family and Couples Education.

4-63 WQ: Sheindlin, Judge Judy. *Keep It Simple, Stupid: You're Smarter Than You Look*, p. 177. Cliff Street Books, New York, 2000.

4-64 WQ: Ogden Nash quote found at www.smartmarriages.com/marriage.quotes.html. *"Marriage quotes."* Coalition for Marriage, Family and Couples Education.

4-64 SB: *Safe-Talking Game Plan* adapted from Stanley, et al. *A Lasting Promise*, p. 76-82.

4-65 MF: Kulig, Nanci. *"You can work it out: Staying married could be the happiest solution,"* Prevention Magazine, Jan 2003.

4-65 WQ: Graham, Billy. *Just As I Am: The Autobiography of Billy Graham*, p. 714. HarperCollins Publishers, New York, 1997.

4-66 WQ: Iris Krasnow quote from Rockey-Fleming, Alexandria. *"A decade of marriage: Those who reach their 10-year anniversary have cleared many hurdles,"* The Washington Times, May 18, 2003.

4-66 WQ: Tim Hudson quote found at www.smartmarriages.com/marriage.quotes.html. *"Marriage quotes."* Coalition for Marriage, Family and Couples Education.

4-67 WQ: Will Rogers quotes found at www.smartmarriages.com/marriage.quotes.html. *"Marriage quotes."* Coalition for Marriage, Family and Couples Education.

4-67 WQ: Anonymous quote found at www.thinkexist.com/quotations/men_and_women.html *"Men and Women quotes."* ThinkExist.com Quotations Online.

Section FIVE

5-71 SB: Author unknown. *"Hollywood's Happy Couples,"* People Magazine, June 22, 1998.

5-71 SB: Barbara Dafoe Whitehead coined the phrase "divorce culture" in an Atlantic Monthly article entitled, *"Dan Quayle was Right,"* April 1993.

5-72-74 SB: *Choices that Breed Marriage Barriers* adapted from Stanley, et al. *A Lasting Promise*, p. 19-23.

5-75 WQ: Bill Cosby quote found at www.thinkexist.com/quotations/men_and_women.html *"Men and Women quotes."* ThinkExist.com Quotations Online.

5-76 SB: The graph showing levels of intimacy adapted from a presentation at the Marriage Encounter weekend conducted by Life-Trac Family Ministries, Leavenoworth, Washington, November 1998.

5-76 MF: Ibid. Waite and Gallagher. *The Case for Marriage*, p. 74-75.

5-77 WQ: Reiser, Paul. *Couplehood*, p. 210-211. Bantam Books, New York, 1995.

5-77 MF: Ibid. Waite and Gallagher. *The Case for Marriage*, p. 74-75.

5-77 WQ: Ibid. Bennett. *The Broken Hearth*, p 185.

5-78-5-79 SB: *The Choice to Protect Friendship* adapted from Stanley, et al. *A Lasting Promise*, p. 239-245.

5-78 WQ: Martin Luther quote found at www.thinkexist.com/quotations/men_and_women.html *"Men and Women quotes."* ThinkExist.com Quotations Online.

5-78 WQ: Frank Pittman quote found at www.smartmarriages.com/marriage.quotes.html. *"Marriage quotes."* Coalition for Marriage, Family and Couples Education.

5-79 WQ: Aristotle quote found at www.thinkexist.com/quotations/men_and_women.html *"Men and Women quotes."* ThinkExist.com Quotations Online.

5-79 WQ: Weber, Linda, et al. *Promises Promises: Understanding and Encouraging Your Husband*, p. 104. Vision House Publishing, Inc., Gresham, Oregon, 1996.

5-80 SB: *The Choice to Forgive* adapted from Stanley, et al. *A Lasting Promise*, p. 213-217.

5-81 WQ: Rosberg, Dr. Gary, Barbara Rosberg. *Divorce Proof Your Marriage*, p. 75-76. Tyndale House Publishing, Inc., Wheaton, Illinois, 2002.

5-81 WQ: Linda Miles quote found at www.thenewmarriage.com. Linda Miles, Ph.D. and Robert Miles, M.D.

Section SIX

6-86 SB (Attitudes): Fagan, Patrick F. *"Why Religion Matters: The Impact of Religious Practices on Social Stability,"* Backgrounder #1064 by Heritage Foundation. June 25, 1996. Larson, Susan S. *"Spirituality can aid stability of marriage,"* Research News in Science and Theology, May 2003.

6-86 SB (Behaviors): Larson, Peter J. and David H. Olson. *"Spiritual Beliefs and Marriage: A National Survey Based on ENRICH,"* www.lifeinnovations.com. Life Innovations, Inc. Browning, Don S. and Gloria G. Rodriguez. *Reweaving the Social Tapestry: Toward a Public Philosophy and Policy.* p. 99-100. W.W. Norton and Company, Inc. New York, 2002.

6-86 SB (Well-Being): Ibid. Fagan. *"Why Religion Matters."* Browning and Rodriguez, p. 99. Larson. *"Spirituality can aid stability of marriage."*

6-86 WQ: Ibid. Lewis, p. 199-200.

6-87 MF: Ibid. Browning and Rodriguez, p. 99-100.

6-87 MF: Barna Research Group. *"Protestants, Catholics and Mormons Reflect Diverse Levels of Religious Activity,"* July 9, 2001.

6-89 MF: Ibid. Barna Research Group. *"Protestants, Catholics and Mormons."*

6-90 MF: Ibid. Barna Research Group. *"Protestants, Catholics and Mormons."*

6-90 WQ: Foster, Richard J. *Celebration of Discipline: The Path to Spiritual Growth*, 158-159. HarperCollins Publishers, San Francisco, 1988.

6-91 MF: REV! Magazine. April/May 2003.

6-94 WQ: Peter Marshall quote from Marshall, Catherine. *A Man Called Peter: The Story of Peter Marshall*, p. 59. McGraw-Hill Book Company, Inc., New York, 1951.

6-95 WQ: McGraw, Phillip C. *Relationship Rescue: A Seven-Step Strategy for Reconnecting With Your Partner*, p. 244-245. Hyperion, New York, 2000.

6-95 WQ: Bill Cosby quote found at www.thinkexist.com/quotations/men_and_women.html *"Men and Women quotes."* ThinkExist.com Quotations Online.

6-96 WQ: Ibid. Larson. *"Spirituality can aid stability of marriage."*

6-97 WQ: Green, Keith. *"Everything You Should Know Before Getting a Divorce,"* www.lastdayministries.org. Last Day Ministries.

Section SEVEN
7-102 WQ: Harold Lindsell quote from Strober, Gerald S. Graham, *A Day in Billy's Life*, p. 98. Spire Books, Old Tappan, New Jersey, 1976.
7-103 WQ: Ibid. Warren, p. 312.
7-104 WQ: Antoine De Saint-Exupery quote found at www.smartmarriages.com/marriagequotes. html. *"Marriage quotes."* Coalition for Marriage, Family and Couples Education.
7-104 WQ: Medved, Michael and Diane Medved. *Saving Childhood: Protecting Our Children from the National Assault on Innocence*, p. 198. HarperCollins Publishers, Inc., New York, 1998.
7-107 WQ: Billy Joel quote from Associated Press, *"Billy Joel to rent NYC apartment,"* Associated Press. September 16, 2002.
7-107 WQ: Weiner-Davis, Michele. *Divorce Busting*, p. 94. Summit Books, New York, 1992.
7-108 WQ: Blue, Ron and Judy Blue. *Money Talks and So Can We*, p. 54. Zondervan Publishing House, Grand Rapids, Michigan, 1999.
7-112 MF: Ibid. Blue, p. 64.
7-114 WQ: Henry Ford quote found at www.smartmarriages.com/marriagequotes.html. *"Marriage quotes."* Coalition for Marriage, Family and Couples Education.

Section EIGHT
8-121 WQ: Ibid. Foster, p. 43-44.
8-121 WQ: Ibid. Colson, p. 325.
8-122 MF: Michael, Robert T., John H. Gagnon, Edward O. Laumann, and Gina Kolata. *Sex in America: A Definitive Survey*, p. 150. Little, Brown & Company, Toronto, Canada, 1994.
8-123 MF: Ibid. Michael, et al., p. 156.
8-123 WQ: Judith Wallerstein quote from Arp, David and Claudia, and Curt and Natalie Brown. *10 Great Dates Before You Say 'I Do,'* p. 99. Zondervan, Grand Rapids, Michigan, 2003.
8-123 WQ: Jerry Seinfeld quote from Marriage Magazine, p 28. September/October 2001.
8-124 MF: Ibid. Michael, et al., p. 124-125.
8-124 WQ: Ibid. Waite and Gallagher, p. 96.
8-125 WQ: Ibid. McGraw, p. 54.
8-126 MF: Ibid. Michael, et al., p. 119.
8-126 WQ: Ibid. Stanton, p. 44.
8-126 MF: Ibid. Michael, et al., p. 112.
8-127 WQ: Ibid. Bennett, p. 177.

New International Version Bible Verses

Verses cited throughout *Before "I Do"* are from *The Message: The Bible in Contemporary Language*. For your convenience and for those who prefer, the verses used in each section are provided below in today's most popular translation, *The Holy Bible, New International Version*.

Section ONE

"Then God said, 'Let us make man in our image, in our likeness, and let them rule over the fish of the sea and the birds of the air, over the livestock, over all the earth, and over all the creatures that move along the ground.' So God created man in His own image, in the image of God He created him; male and female He created them."
Genesis 1:26-27

"God blessed them and said to them, 'Be fruitful and increase in number; fill the earth and subdue it.'"
Genesis 1:28a

"'Rule over the fish of the sea and the birds of the air and over every living creature that moves on the ground.' Then God said, 'I give you every seed-bearing plant on the face of the whole earth and every tree that has fruit with seed in it. They will be yours for food. And to all the beasts of the earth and all the birds of the air and all the creatures that move on the ground—everything that has the breath of life in it—I give every green plant for food.' And it was so. God saw all that he had made, and it was very good. And there was evening, and there was morning—the sixth day."
Genesis 1:28b-31

"The Lord God said, 'It is not good for the man to be alone. I will make a helper suitable for him.'

Now the Lord God had formed out of the ground all the beasts of the field and all the birds of the air. He brought them to the man to see what he would name them; and whatever the man called each living creature, that was its name. So the man gave names to all the livestock, the birds of the air and all the beasts of the field.

But for Adam no suitable helper was found. So the Lord God caused the man to fall into a deep sleep; and while he was sleeping, He took one of the man's ribs and closed up the place with flesh. Then the Lord God made a woman from the rib He had taken out of the man, and He brought her to the man.

The man said, 'This is now bone of my bones and flesh of my flesh; she shall be called 'woman,' for she was taken out of man.' For this reason a man will leave his father and mother and be united to his wife, and they will become one flesh. The man and his wife were both naked, and they felt no shame."
Genesis 2:18-25

"Love must be sincere. Hate what is evil; cling to what is good. Be devoted to one another in brotherly love. Honor one another above yourselves."
Romans 12:9-10

"Now that you have purified yourselves by obeying the truth so that you have sincere love for your brothers, love one another deeply, from the heart."
I Peter 1:22

"I belong to my lover and his desire is for me."
 Song of Solomon 7:10

"Come, my lover, let us go to the countryside, let us spend the night in the villages. Let us go into vineyards to see if the vines have budded, if their blossoms have opened and if the pomegranates are in bloom - there I will give you my love."
 Song of Solomon 7:11-12

"Dear friends, let us love one another, for love comes from God. Everyone who loves has been born of God and knows God. Whoever does not love does not know God, because God is love. This is how God showed his love among us: He sent his one and only Son into the world that we might live through him. This is love: not that we loved God, but that he loved us and sent his Son as an atoning sacrifice for our sins. Dear friends, since God so loved us, we also ought to love one another."
I John 4:7-11

"Love is patient, love is kind. It does not envy, it does not boast, it is not proud. It is not rude, it is not self-seeking, it is not easily angered, it keeps no record of wrongs. Love does not delight in evil but rejoices with the truth. It always protects, always trusts, always hopes, always perseveres. Love never fails."
I Corinthians 13:4-8a

"When a man makes a vow to the Lord or takes an oath to obligate himself by a pledge, he must not break his word but must do everything he said."
Numbers 30:2

"Whatever your lips utter you must be sure to do, because you made your vow freely to the Lord your God with your own mouth."
Deuteronomy 23:23

"It is a trap for a man to dedicate something rashly and only later to consider his vows."
Proverbs 20:25

"...the Lord is acting as the witness between you and the wife of your youth...she is your partner, the wife of your marriage covenant. Has not the Lord made them one? In flesh and spirit they are His. And why one? Because He was seeking godly offspring. So guard yourself in your spirit, and do not break faith with the wife of your youth."
Malachi 2:14-15

"When you are making a vow to God, do not delay in fulfilling it. He has no pleasure in fools; fulfill your vow. It is better not to vow than to make a vow and not fulfill it. Do not let your mouth lead you into sin. And do not protest to the temple messenger, 'My vow was a mistake.' Why should God be angry at what you say and destroy the works of your hands? Much dreaming and many words are meaningless. Therefore stand in awe of God."
Ecclesiastes 5:4-7

Section TWO
"The Lord God said, 'It is not good for the man to be alone. I will make a helper suitable for him.'

Now the Lord God had formed out of the ground all the beasts of the field and all the birds of the air. He brought them to the man to see what he would name them; and whatever the man called each living creature, that was its name. So the man gave names to all the livestock, the birds of the air and all the beasts of the field. But for Adam no suitable helper was found. So the Lord God caused the man to fall into a deep sleep; and while he was sleeping, He took one of the man's ribs and closed up the place with flesh. Then the Lord God made a woman from the rib He had taken out of the man, and He brought her to the man.

The man said, 'This is now bone of my bones and flesh of my flesh; she shall be called woman, for she was taken out of man.' For this reason a man will leave his father and mother and be united to his wife, and they will become one flesh."
Genesis 2:18-24

"For You created my inmost being; You knit me together in my mother's womb. I praise You because I am fearfully and wonderfully made; Your works are wonderful, I know that full well. My frame was not hidden from You when I was made in the secret place. When I was woven together in the depths of the earth, Your eyes saw my unformed body. All the days ordained for me were written in Your book before one of them came to be."
Psalm 139:13-16

"The Lord is my shepherd, I shall not be in want. He makes me lie down in green pastures, He leads me beside quiet waters, He restores my soul. He guides me in paths of righteousness for His name's sake. Even though I walk through the valley of the shadow of death, I will fear no evil, for You are with me; Your rod and Your staff, they comfort me."
Psalm 23:1-4

Section THREE

"'Haven't you read,' he (Jesus) replied, 'that at the beginning the Creator 'made them male and female,' and said, 'For this reason a man will leave his father and mother and be united to his wife, and the two will become one flesh'? So they are no longer two, but one. Therefore what God has joined together, let man not separate.'"
Matthew 19:4-6

"Now I want you to realize that the head of every man is Christ, and the head of the woman is man, and the head of Christ is God ... In the Lord, however, woman is not independent of man, nor is man independent of woman. For as woman came from man, so also man is born of woman. But everything comes from God."
I Corinthians 11:3, 11-12

"Submit to one another out of reverence for Christ. Wives, submit to your husbands as to the Lord. For the husband is the head of the wife as Christ is the head of the church, his body, of which he is the Savior. Now as the church submits to Christ, so also wives should submit to their husbands in everything."
Ephesians 5:21-24

"Husbands, in the same way be considerate as you live with your wives, and treat them with respect as the weaker partner and as heirs with you of the gracious gift of life, so that nothing will hinder your prayers."
I Peter 3:7

"Husbands, love your wives, just as Christ loved the church and gave himself up for her ..."
Ephesians 5:25

"Fathers, do not exasperate your children; instead, bring them up in the training and instruction of the Lord."
Ephesians 6:4

"Husbands, love your wives, just as Christ loved the church and gave himself up for her to make her holy, cleansing her by the washing with water through the word, and to present her to himself as a radiant church, without stain or wrinkle or any other blemish, but holy and blameless. In this same way, husbands ought to love their wives as their own bodies. He who loves his wife loves himself. After all, no one ever hated his own body, but he feeds and cares for it, just as Christ does for the church."
Ephesians 5:25-29

"This is a profound mystery – but I am talking about Christ and the church. However, each one of you also must love his wife as he loves himself, and the wife must respect her husband."
Ephesians 5:32-33

"Husbands, love your wives and do not be harsh with them."
Colossians 3:19

"The Lord God said, 'It is not good for the man to be alone. I will make a helper suitable for him.'"
Genesis 2:18

"A wife of noble character who can find? She is worth more than rubies. Her husband has full confidence in her and lacks nothing of value. She brings him good, not harm, all the days of her life ... She watches over the affairs of her household and does not eat the bread of idleness. Her children arise and call her blessed; her husband also, and he praises her: 'Many women do noble things but you surpass them all.'"
Proverbs 31:10-12; 27-29

"So I counsel younger widows to marry, to have children, to manage their homes and to give the enemy no opportunity for slander."
I Timothy 5:14

"Then they (older women) can train the younger women to love their husbands and children, to be self-controlled and pure, to be busy at home, to be kind, and to be subject to their husbands, so that no one will malign the word of God."
Titus 2:4-5

"This is a profound mystery – but I am talking about Christ and the church. However, each one of you also must love his wife as he loves himself, and the wife must respect her husband."
Ephesians 5:32-33

Section FOUR

"What causes fights and quarrels among you? Don't they come from your desires that battle within you? You want something but don't get it. You kill and covet, but you cannot have what you want. You quarrel and fight. You do not have, because you do not ask God. When you ask, you do not receive, because you ask with wrong motives, that you may spend what you get on your pleasures."
James 4:1-3

"Reckless words pierce like a sword, but the tongue of the wise brings healing."
Proverbs 12:18

"He who answers before listening – that is his folly and shame."
Proverbs 18:13

"A fool shows his annoyance at once, but a prudent man overlooks an insult."
Proverbs 12:16

"Stop listening to instruction, my son, and you will stray from the words of knowledge."
Proverbs 19:27

"Therefore judge nothing before the appointed time; wait till the Lord comes. He will bring to light what is hidden in darkness and will expose the motives of men's hearts. At that time each will receive his praise from God."
I Corinthians 4:5

"If anyone considers himself religious and yet does not keep a tight rein on his tongue, he deceives himself and his religion is worthless."
James 1:26

"But I tell you that anyone who is angry with his brother will be subject to judgment. Again, anyone who says to his brother, 'Raca,' is answerable to the Sanhedrin. But anyone who says, 'You fool!' will be in danger of the fire of hell."
Matthew 5:22

"My dear brothers, take note of this: Everyone should be quick to listen, slow to speak and slow to become angry, for man's anger does not bring about the righteous life God desires."
James 1:19-20

"Therefore each of you must put off falsehood and speak truthfully to his neighbor, for we are all members of one body. 'In your anger do not sin': Do not let the sun go down while you are still angry, and do not give the devil a foothold."
Ephesians 4:25-27

"Two are better than one, because they have a good return for their work: If one falls down, his friend can help him up. But pity the man who falls and has no one to help him up! Also, if two lie down together, they will keep warm. But how can one keep warm alone? Though one may be overpowered, two can defend themselves. A cord of three strands is not quickly broken."
Ecclesiastes 4:9-12

Section FIVE

"When the woman saw that the fruit of the tree was good for food and pleasing to the eye, and also desirable for gaining wisdom, she took some and ate it. She also gave some to her husband, who was with her, and he ate it. Then the eyes of both of them were opened, and they realized they were naked; so they sewed fig leaves together and made coverings for themselves.

Then the man and his wife heard the sound of the Lord God as He was walking in the garden in the cool of the day, and they hid from the Lord God among the trees of the garden. But the Lord God called to the man, 'Where are you?' He answered, 'I heard you in the garden, and I was afraid because I was naked; so I hid.'

And He said, 'Who told you that you were naked? Have you eaten from the tree that I commanded you not to eat from?' The man said, 'The woman you put here with me—she gave me some fruit from the tree, and I ate it.'

Then the Lord God said to the woman, 'What is this you have done?' The woman said, 'The serpent deceived me, and I ate.'"
Genesis 3:6-13

"Two are better than one, because they have a good return for their work: If one falls down, his friend can help him up. But pity the man who falls and has no one to help him up! Also, if two lie down together, they will keep warm. But how can one keep warm alone? Though one may be overpowered, two can defend themselves. A cord of three strands is not quickly broken."
Ecclesiastes 4:9-12

"Do not repay evil with evil or insult with insult, but with blessing, because to this you were called so that you may inherit a blessing. For, 'Whoever would love life and see good days must keep his tongue from evil and his lips from deceitful speech. He must turn from evil and do good; he must seek peace and pursue it.'"
I Peter 3:9-11

"Bear with each other and forgive whatever grievances you may have against one another. Forgive as the Lord forgave you."
Colossians 3:13

Section SIX
"Therefore, I urge you, brothers, in view of God's mercy, to offer your bodies as living sacrifices, holy and pleasing to God – this is your spiritual act of worship. Do not conform any longer to the pattern of this world, but be transformed by the renewing of your mind. Then you will be able to test and approve what God's will is – his good, pleasing and perfect will."
Romans 12:1-2

"What good is it, my brothers, if a man claims to have faith but has no deeds? Can such faith save him? Suppose a brother or sister is without clothes and daily food. If one of you says to him, 'Go, I wish you well; keep warm and well fed,' but does nothing about his physical needs, what good is it? In the same way, faith by itself, if it is not accompanied by action, is dead.

But someone will say, 'You have faith; I have deeds.' Show me your faith without deeds, and I will show you my faith by what I do. You believe that there is one God. Good! Even the demons believe that – and shudder. You foolish man, do you want evidence that faith without deeds is useless? … You see that a person is justified by what he does and not by faith alone."
James 2:14-20, 24

"Husbands, in the same way be considerate as you live with your wives, and treat them with respect as the weaker partner and as heirs with you of the gracious gift of life, so that nothing will hinder your prayers."
I Peter 3:7

"Another thing you do: You flood the Lord's altar with tears. You weep and wail because He no longer pays attention to Your offerings or accepts them with pleasure from your hands. You ask, 'Why?' It is because the Lord is acting as the witness between you and the wife of your youth, because you have broken faith with her, though she is your partner, the wife of your marriage covenant. Has not the Lord made them one? In flesh and spirit they are His. And why one? Because He was seeking godly offspring. So guard yourself in your spirit, and do not break faith with the wife of your youth.

'I hate divorce,' says the Lord God of Israel, 'and I hate a man's covering himself with violence as well as with his garment,' says the Lord Almighty. So guard yourself in your spirit, and do not break faith."
Malachi 2:13-16

"Let the word of Christ dwell in you richly as you teach and admonish one another with all wisdom, and as you sing psalms, hymns and spiritual songs with gratitude in your hearts to God."
Colossians 3:16

"Do not be anxious about anything, but in everything, by prayer and petition, with thanksgiving, present your requests to God. And the peace of God, which transcends all understanding, will guard your hearts and your minds in Christ Jesus."
Philippians 4:6-7

"Therefore, my dear friends, as you have always obeyed – not only in my presence, but now much more in my absence – continue to work out your salvation with fear and trembling, for it is God who works in you to will and to act according to His good purpose."
Philippians 2:12-13

"Since, then, you have been raised with Christ, set your hearts on things above, where Christ is seated at the right hand of God. Set your minds on things above, not on earthly things. For you died, and your life is now hidden with Christ in God."
Colossians 3:1-3

Section SEVEN
"Whoever trusts in his riches will fall, but the righteous will thrive like a green leaf."
Proverbs 11:28

"In Him we were also chosen, having been predestined according to the plan of Him who works out everything in conformity with the purpose of His will."
Ephesians 1:11

"Consider it pure joy, my brothers, whenever you face trials of many kinds, because you know that the testing of your faith develops perseverance. "
James 1:2-3

"The earth is the Lord's, and everything in it, the world, and all who live in it."
Psalm 24:1

"But godliness with contentment is great gain. For we brought nothing into the world, and we can take nothing out of it. But if we have food and clothing, we will be content with that."
I Timothy 6:6-8

"And God is able to make all grace abound to you, so that in all things at all times, having all that you need, you will abound in every good work. As it is written: 'He has scattered abroad His gifts to the poor; His righteousness endures forever.' Now He who supplies seed to the sower and bread for food will also supply and increase your store of seed and will enlarge the harvest of your righteousness."
II Corinthians 9:8-10

"Do not store up for yourselves treasures on earth, where moth and rust destroy, and where thieves break in and steal. But store up for yourselves treasures in heaven, where moth and rust do not destroy, and where thieves do not break in and steal."
Matthew 6:19-20

"People who want to get rich fall into temptation and a trap and into many foolish and harmful desires that plunge men into ruin and destruction. For the love of money is a root of all kinds of evil. Some people, eager for money, have wandered from the faith and pierced themselves with many griefs."
I Timothy 6:9-10

"Do not wear yourself out to get rich; have the wisdom to show restraint. Cast but a glance at riches, and they are gone, for they will surely sprout wings and fly off to the sky like an eagle."
Proverbs 23:4-5

"Command those who are rich in this present world not to be arrogant nor to put their hope in wealth, which is so uncertain, but to put their hope in God, who richly provides us with everything for our enjoyment. Command them to do good, to be rich in good deeds, and to be generous and willing to share. In this way they will lay up treasure for themselves as a firm foundation for the coming age, so that they may take hold of the life that is truly life."
I Timothy 6:17-19

"Honor the Lord with your wealth, with the firstfruits of all your crops."
Proverbs 3:9

"'Consider carefully what you hear,' he (Jesus) continued. 'With the measure you use, it will be measured to you – and even more. Whoever has will be given more; whoever does not have, even what he has will be taken from him.'"
Mark 4:24-25

Section EIGHT

"Like an apple tree among the trees of the forest is my lover among the young men. I delight to sit in his shade, and his fruit is sweet to my taste. He has taken me to the banquet hall, and his banner over me is love."
Song of Solomon 2:3-4

"My lover is mine and I am his; he browses among the lilies. Until the day breaks and the shadows flee, turn, my lover, and be like a gazelle or like a young stag on the rugged hills."
Song of Solomon 2:16-17

"Daughters of Jerusalem, I charge you by the gazelles and by the does of the field: Do not arouse or awaken love until it so desires."
Song of Solomon 3:5

"Come out, you daughters of Zion, and look at King Solomon wearing the crown, the crown with which his mother crowned him on the day of his wedding, the day his heart rejoiced."
Song of Solomon 3:11

"You are a garden fountain, a well of flowing water streaming down from Lebanon. Awake, north wind, and come, south wind! Blow on my garden, that its fragrance may spread abound. Let my lover come into his garden and taste its choice fruits."
Song of Solomon 4:15-16

"I have come into my garden, my sister, my bride; I have gathered my myrrh with my spice. I have eaten my honeycomb and my honey; I have drunk my wine and my milk. Eat, O friends, and drink; drink your fill, O lovers."
Song of Solomon 5:1

"I belong to my lover, and his desire is for me."
Song of Solomon 7:10

"Marriage should be honored by all, and the marriage bed kept pure, for God will judge the adulterer and all the sexually immoral."
Hebrews 13:4

"Finally, brothers, we instructed you how to live in order to please God, as in fact you are living. Now we ask you and urge you in the Lord Jesus to do this more and more. For you know what instructions we gave you by the authority of the Lord Jesus.

It is God's will that you should be sanctified: that you should avoid sexual immorality; that each of you should learn to control his own body in a way that is holy and honorable, not in passionate lust like the heathen, who do not know God; and that in this matter no one should wrong his brother or take advantage of him. The Lord will punish men for all such sins, as we have already told you and warned you.

For God did not call us to be impure, but to live a holy life. Therefore, he who rejects this instruction does not reject man but God, who gives you His Holy Spirit."
I Thessalonians 4:1-8

"Drink water from your own cistern, running water from your own well. Should your springs overflow in the streets, your streams of water in the public squares? Let them be yours alone, never to be shared with strangers.

May your fountain be blessed, and may you rejoice in the wife of your youth. A loving doe, a graceful deer—may her breasts satisfy you always, may you ever be captivated by her love."
Proverbs 5:15-19

"Now for the matters you wrote about: It is good for a man not to marry. But since there is so much immorality, each man should have his own wife, and each woman her own husband. The husband should fulfill his marital duty to his wife, and likewise the wife to her husband. The wife's body does not belong to her alone but also to her husband. In the same way, the husband's body does not belong to him alone but also to his wife.

Do not deprive each other except by mutual consent and for a time, so that you may devote yourselves to prayer. Then come together again so that Satan will not tempt you because of your lack of self-control. I say this as a concession, not as a command."
I Corinthians 7:1-6

"God blessed them and said to them, 'Be fruitful and increase in number; fill the earth and subdue it."
Genesis 1:28

"If we claim to be without sin, we deceive ourselves and the truth is not in us. If we confess our sins, He is faithful and just and will forgive us our sins and purify us from all unrighteousness."
1 John 1:8-9

"Cast all your anxiety upon Him because He cares for you."
1 Peter 5:7

About the Author

K. Jason Krafsky's life mission is to help couples experience all marriage has to offer, and live the *Full Marriage Experience*.

He has spent many years helping communities and churches prepare couples for marriage, enrich marriages, and mend hurting marriages. Through his work with Families Northwest, Jason has trained community, faith, and government leaders to advance marriage and family efforts aimed at turning the tide of family breakdown.

Jason's unique expertise in developing community based marriage-strengthening activities made him a nationally recognized leader in the marriage movement. He is involved with the Coalition for Marriage, Family and Couple Education, the Association of Marriage and Family Ministries, the Marriage CoMission, and the Marriage Movement. He has had the privilege to serve as a contracted consultant to one of the nation's first federally funded Community Healthy Marriage Initiatives.

Jason has spoken on both local and national radio and TV programs, and has been featured in various newspaper articles.

Over the years, Jason has acted as a relationship coach for engaged couples, and spoken at numerous marriage enrichment events. He has been trained in various relationship strengthening tools including PREPARE/ENRICH, FOCCUS/REFOCCUS, and PREP.

Jason is ordained at New Community Church in Maple Valley, Washington and serves on the teaching team. He has held ministry positions at various churches in the Seattle area, including pastor-in-training at Overlake Christian Church, discipleship pastor at Coal Creek Chapel, church planter with Pacific Christian Fellowship of House Churches, and shepherding elder at Harbor Fellowship. He graduated from Northwest College with a major in Biblical Literature and a minor in Communications.

Jason was raised in the Northwest, where he now resides with his wife, Kelli, and their four children (Caleb, Jaelyn, Josh, and Cole), in the foothills of Washington's Cascade Mountains.

Jason is available for a variety of consulting and speaking engagements, including:

    -- Speaking at special events
    -- Teaching at couples conferences
    -- Preaching at church services
    -- Consulting community marriage initiatives
    -- Coaching church marriage & family ministries

Requests can be sent to kjasonk@FullMarriageExperience.com or by calling 425.432.TIDE (8433).

Order More Books Today!

Before "I Do"

Preparing for the Full Marriage Experience

This in-depth, interactive book prepares couples to go the distance and experience all marriage has to offer.

Couples, get married with confidence, assurance, and purpose! Whether you are engaged, pre-engaged, or newly married, prepare to live the *Full Marriage Experience* by reading this in-depth, interactive guide.

Pastors, supply pre-married couples with everything they need to know for a healthy, lifelong marriage (with no extra effort or training on your part)! *Before "I Do"* is ideal for your church's premarital program, and complements the PREPARE or FOCCUS inventories.

Parents, help your child and their prospective spouse eliminate common relationship obstacles, obtain the practical skills, and frame their relationship with God's insights. *Before "I Do"* will help them build the foundation for a lasting marriage.

Mentor couples, this is the resource you have been looking for! Relieve the pressure of feeling like you need to "know it all." This book makes your time with younger couples fresh, informative, and fun.

ISBN: 0-9769556-0-1

PRICING & ORDERING

One copy is $24.95 (plus $5 shipping and handling, and $2.10 sales tax if applicable*).
Two or more copies... go to www.FullMarriageExperience.com for special bulk pricing.
*Washington residents, 8.4% added for sales tax.

Billing

Organization _____
Name _____
Address _____
City / State _____
Zip Code _____
Day Phone _____
E-Mail _____
Credit Card # _____
Name on Card _____
Card Number _____
Expiration _____
Today's Date _____

Shipping *(if different than Billing)*

Organization _____
Name _____
Address _____
City / State _____
Zip Code _____
Day Phone _____
E-Mail _____

☐ **I have enclosed a check payable to: Turn the Tide Resource Group, LLC.**

☐ **Please charge my credit card.**

Mail completed form and payment to:
Turn the Tide Resource Group, LLC
26828 Maple Valley Hwy #260
Maple Valley, WA 98038

Order online at: www.FullMarriageExperience.com

Turn
the
Tide
resource group

425.432.TIDE (8433)